The Trophy Striper

Frank Daignault

Edited by Joyce Daignault

 BURFORD BOOKS

Also by Frank Daignault

Twenty Years on the Cape: My Time as a Surfcaster

Striper Surf

Striper Hot Spots: The 100 Top Surfcasting Locations from New Jersey to Maine

Photo on p. 61 courtesy Charles E. Cinto; p. 121 courtesy Dick Alley; p. 135, 136 courtesy Kay Townsend; p. 144 courtesy Tim Coleman; p. 162 Stuart Jones; all other photos by Joyce Daignault, Dick Daignault, or the author.

Library of Congress Cataloging-in-Publication Data
Daignault, Frank, 1936–
The trophy striper / by Frank Daignault.
      p.   cm.
   ISBN 1–58080–040–8 (pb.)
   1. Striped bass fishing.   I. Title.
SH691.S7D36   1999
799.1'7732—dc21
                                    99–32060
                                      CIP

Contents

Preface

WE ARE AT THE THRESHOLD of another period of monster linesides. And because of this size-enhanced fishery, surfcasting is no longer limited to fishing for small stripers. There is a big difference between the fish-on-every-cast throwbacks most of you trained on and the moby bass with which many of you will soon be confronted. Thus, this book will examine all of the influences that come into play when you're fishing for large striped bass from the surf. I'll also examine the angling dynamics with which you'll be confronted as a surfcaster, because they are profoundly different from those associated with fishing in boats.

In the striper moratorium that arose from the conservation concerns of the 1980s, size limits were purposely raised to protect the available stripers of the time. A result was that the bass caught were nearly always too small to be taken, and a keeper became as much a rarity as sizable stripers once had been. This carrot-on-a-stick situation redefined a "keeper" while dramatizing the notion that truly big stripers might either be out there or in the cards at some future time. A premoratorium lineside might have been big enough to keep at 16 inches; this crept higher and higher all through the late 1980s and early 1990s until the minimum requirement in most states was 36 inches—a fish that, on average, weighed 18 pounds.

The recovery of striped bass in the northwestern Atlantic is the wildlife restoration success of our time. Population projections for the dominant southern stocks—based not upon models, but upon young-of-the-year indices—show that we have had 2 reproductive seasons in the last 10, ending in 1997, that exceeded the 50-year all-

One of seven 50-pound-plus trophy stripers beached in my lifetime in the striper surf.

time high of 1970; 4 other years yielded well above average. While no one knows what lies in the reproductive cards, we are unlikely to lose what was born and most likely to enjoy previously unknown levels of fishable stripers. The consequence of such robust numbers is strong interest in sport fishing for the species. Evolution from concern for catching large numbers to concern for catching big ones is both a natural progression and a reasonable expectation for anglers. Of course at this writing we can still safely blame our inability to find trophy stripers regularly upon what was not born a suitable number of years ago. That will change. Soon students of the striper surf will encounter dream fish, a "two-hands-to-carry" level of angling achievement, stripers well past, in the words of my New Hampshire cornball pal, "keepahs."

I've fished the beach for 40 years. I learned something about how to fish for big fish back in the glory days of stripering. Few of us remain from that time when I fished as a kid on the beach. Then, I learned the nuances that exemplify the behavior of what we call cows. I bring this to you now because we are approaching a new era of opportunity, a greater period for huge bass than is likely in living memory.

Cinch a belt around your oilskins, check your drag, and note the wind. Let's go fishing on my storied striper coast for trophy stripers.

Acknowledgments

IN A PERFECT boy-meets-girl world, he would gather bait, she would pack a lunch, and together they would take a canoe to drift for smallmouths. As lines tightened, each of them would hope for the other to catch a frisky gamester that would validate their efforts and intensify their bonding. Soon after, they would marry, have beautiful children—not always one at a time—and negotiate the obstacle course of life. In this consummate world their bonds would grow in all their pursuits, from college to friendly analysis of literary interests—all punctuated by children's diseases and incessant poverty.

How ideal could the world be if he did not have another who would care for his children, revel in his accomplishments, grieve in his disappointments, and share in his moments of sadness? I have often wondered what it would be like to pursue bucks in the hardwoods, pheasants rising from a frost-rimmed meadow, lakers on a wildwood shore, and stripers on a wind beach . . . alone. At times I have even grieved for those whose lovers failed to appreciate these joys. Perfection dictates that we share all of what make life's wines more agreeable with our high school sweetheart.

To Joyce, who has given love.

—Frank Daignault, September 1999

ONE

Beyond the Keeper

THE OPPORTUNITY for a big striper does not lie in your talents, work ethic, methods, friends, or resourcefulness; rather, the chance springs from what is there. And what is there is based upon what was born in the preceding years—a highly variable yet moderately well-known quantity: population. The population of striper-coast fish is made up of three major groups and an unknown number of lesser fisheries. In order of size these are the southern—the true bellwether of opportunity—Virginia and Maryland migrants that add up to around 90 percent of our total; the Hudson River fishery, believed to rank second in size; and the more recent Delaware River fishery, a race of bass that have enjoyed late restoration because of better environmental controls at tidewater. Smaller fisheries, such as Maine's Kennebec—which is the most exciting of the small ones— are scattered from Connecticut to the Maritimes.

The two largest sources of stripers in our northwestern Atlantic each use a scientific means of measuring the spawn of the season

Juvenile stripers like this one project opportunities for 20 years later.

known as the young-of-the-year index (YOY). The crucially important Maryland index is determined by averaging the number of juvenile bass found in three rounds of seining at 22 sites on the Chesapeake Bay; the highest total ever recorded, at this writing, was 59 in 1996; the lowest under 1 in 1981. Fisheries managers generally consider anything above 8 to indicate a good spawning year. This measure of fecundity yields highly variable levels of success for a given season; one year there might be a skillion juvenile bass swimming around and the next only a few. These variations cause dramatic changes in available bass as well as in their sizes from one year to the next. For instance, people from New Jersey to Maine might be catching many 12-inch-shorts from an abundant year-class migrating for the first time. Then a group of 26-inchers from a few years earlier makes an appearance. Such dominant

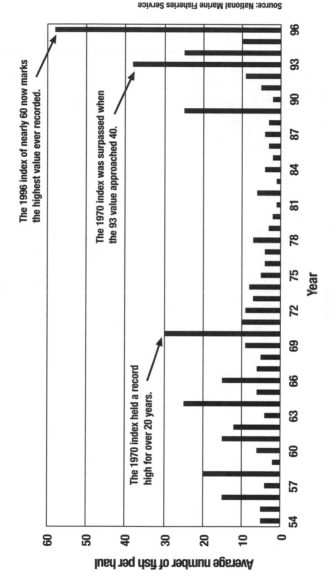

MARYLAND JUVENILE STRIPED BASS SURVEY INDEX

The 1996 index of nearly 60 now marks the highest value ever recorded.

The 1970 index was surpassed when the 93 value approached 40.

The 1970 index held a record high for over 20 years.

Source: National Marine Fisheries Service

Average number of fish per haul

Year

The crucially important Maryland index is determined by averaging the number of juvenile bass found in three rounds of seining at 22 sites on the Chesapeake Bay; the highest ever recorded was 59 in 1996, the lowest under 1 in 1981. Fishery managers generally consider anything above 8 to be a good spawning year. Source: National Marine Fisheries Service and Salt Water Sportsman magazine.

DON'T BELIEVE IT

Even crotchety old-timers have never seen the number of striped bass that swim in our waters these days. A natural consequence is concern for the environment's ability to support these numbers—what the game managers call biobalance. But in truth there is no evidence that linesides have outstripped the environment's ability to support the species. People are citing examples of poor growth that are not poor growth. Try these: A charter skipper with over 30 years of experience laments, "The old rule of thumb of a pound per inch of length no longer applies. I had a thirty-five-inch fish that weighed a miserly seventeen pounds." If you check the chart on page 11, you'll see that in 1970 fish that measured 34 inches weighed 15 pounds; those 38 inches long weighed 18 pounds. Another commentator claims that fish from the good old days that were 40 inches long usually weighed 40 pounds. *They never weighed that much at that length, never.*

Moreover, today's observers, if they're using contemporary methods that measure *total* length, are measuring even smaller bass; the old measurements, as well as world records, used fork length, which is about an inch shorter than total length. Thus, if measured properly and in the same way, a 34-inch bass would have weighed 15 pounds 30 years ago—as it does now. Not only are stripers finding suitable sustenance, but they are exhibiting the same growth potential in the same environment that they've spent a million years evolving to fit.

year-classes bring some predictability to the picture, which comes into focus when everybody is catching from the same good indices. All through the 1990s we caught small bass, because that was what dominated striper stocks. Now we are entering a period of large-striper-fishing opportunity that was last experienced between 1970 and 1980.

The term *keeper* is a postmoratorium (from the late 1980s on) term born from the repeated raising of the size limit of an allowable striper. Keepers had little importance in the old days because, here in the North, few migration-capable bass were throwbacks given a size limit of 16 inches. Recent attention to the term is a natural outgrowth of the continuous contacting of fish up to 18 pounds—which were not suitably legal during some years of the restoration. Also, there is—depending

Rhode Island's Jack Goda with a 58-pounder circa 1968. Opportunity for a big striper varies from year to year, but fish like this will soon be in the cards.

upon what years you speak of—great variation in what constitutes a keeper. With 36-inch fish weighing 18 or so pounds and 28-inch fish weighing half that, both keepers depending upon the year, there is little definition of size to be derived from the term. The next level of striper we should define is the *trophy*. For convenience we can consider this any striper of a size that is larger than what is commonly caught. Today's trophy will be tomorrow's routine encounter, probably until fair numbers of 50-pounders are available. The carrot is again on the stick.

Because all stripers *appear* the same, it is difficult to determine their river of origin—what biologists call stock identification. It is important to know what percentage of our stripers come from what source or stock composition. DNA science makes that determination possible, but no project, at this writing, has yet been undertaken to determine what percentages of migratory stripers from a particular source are found in the total. Old studies believed that 90 percent of stocks were southern, 9 percent were Hudson, and 1 percent all others; no doubt there are some shifts in stock composition as the various fecundity rates of some races of bass vary. We can expect great or small numbers from a particular river's year-class, but the wild card will always be that anomaly fish born in a little-known river of origin or during a "bad" year. Thus, while what most of us are catching is governed by what we think was born, somebody catches a monster from a bad year or from a less important river. This happens just often enough to keep us on our toes and to remind us about how little is known.

In the summer of 1996, a time when every club I knew gave its fish-of-the-year award to a 35-pounder—a lineside born in the southern YOY index of 1982—I heard of five stripers taken from boats in Rhode Island that were over 50 pounds. I think, though there is no way of proving it, that these were Hudson River fish from a year that was bad elsewhere. There will always be wild cards.

Opportunity for a big striper varies from year to year as a result, and with this variability comes a change in the yardstick that measures bigness. In 1990 the moratorium-breaking '82 year-class had people measuring 15-pounders while looking for a keeper. Few were seen that year any bigger. But we knew better than to complain because five years earlier we had nothing for which to fish. In 1997 club-winning fish were in the high 30s. Note that the numbers get better all the time.

Size discussions about stripers now use inches as opposed to pounds. This is a direct result of 10 years of preoccupation with fish that had to be measured. Of course it is understandable—how else are we to determine a lineside's qualifications without hurting it while being pushed and bullied by a raging surf in the deep night? But while inches may work, length is a poor measure of a striper's size. It should

During the moratorium we measured bass like this looking for keepers.

be pounds—the traditional measure—because individual conditions can create dramatic differences between two stripers of the same length. Using a 16-year-old year-class as an example, a 42-inch fish could be as heavy as 38 pounds and as light as 28. Contemporary measurement might call this a tie, but I say that somebody has lost the contest by 10 pounds. The oft-mentioned rule of an inch per pound—using fork length—only becomes valid at around 50 inches. For accuracy, many people today measure total length; the traditional fork length is an inch shorter in bass over 40 inches.

As with mammals, individual condition will define much of a striper's potential in terms of being able to resist, to fight. Thin fish, athletic ones that carry less weight but the same muscle, can put up enough fight to the rod to fool anglers into believing that they have latched onto something way bigger. Such "racers," as they are called, are famous for making experienced surf fishers beg for help in the surf or retch in the dunes if they've dropped them or broken off. Racers fight hard. They win battles, not fishing contests. And the more years that go by, the more disadvantages nature puts in your path toward a trophy striper.

There is widespread belief that racers are males, but in the size range I'm speaking of, most fish over 15 pounds are females. True, some old-timers still refer to outsize bass as bull bass, but they are really cows and this is commonly understood. Male stripers rarely exceed 15 pounds, and books say that the largest buck ever found went to 40. Because half are males, all the conservation practices in the world deny half of the stripers born from ever being outsize. When you take this into account, even if there were never a line or net thrown, all the males of a year-class would be gone after eight or so years.

I'm not really sure how the tradition began, but the most acclaimed measure of a trophy striper is that of 50 pounds. Maybe it was a milestone that combined the right quantities of rarity and possibility. Reporting for the *New York Times* in the fall of 1998, Andrea

Kannapell, while interviewing Scott Parker from Montauk, quoted him about such fish: "A 50-pounder?" he said. "I'd French-kiss it! I already told my wife, 'I catch a 50-pounder, you're out of bed.' I'm making love to that fish for a month!" Tackle companies have given awards for that size, including the old Ashaway Line and Twine's "Nifty Fifty Club." A New York brewery gave awards for such fish for years. And the traditional point at which most striper piscophiles run to the taxidermist is 50 pounds. At any rate, for surfcasters 50-pounders don't come easily. I say surfcasters because, as in all other surf-to-boat comparisons, the boaters will take 10 times the trophies. The golden mark of 50 pounds has always seemed silly to me; I have for years watched people kick the tires of their buggy in distress when

We are entering a period of large-striper-fishing opportunity that was last experienced between 1970 and 1980.

the spring on the scale stopped at 49. They should have had the fish mounted anyway.

The opportunity for such moby stripers has not remained historically constant. I don't think that 20 such fish were caught in 1998 coastwide, boat and surf combined. The greatest known number was around 225 in the late 1960s. And in 1966, 125 were reported. In both years about 10 percent came from the surf. An old Schaefer Brewery Contest report that happened to survive my files summarized the 1967 season with one "73 pounder, 12 sixty pounders, and 139 fifty pounders." Just prior to the fishery's crash there was a historically important season in 1981 during which more 50-pounders were caught than ever before. But the brewery that once maintained such records, criticized for rewarding the slaughter of our biggest stripers, had stopped awarding and stopped counting. So no one knows how many monsters were taken during perhaps the biggest year in striper-fishing history. Examining old records of some of the striper clubs of the time, top fish varied from 42 to 45 pounds in the early 1960s. You could almost see them grow, as we are experiencing today.

Fifty-pounders are, on average, around 20 years old, so keep your eyes open after the year 2000.

This size and age chart lists highly approximated average striper lengths, weights, and ages. Individual variations caused by season, river of origin, and sex make this an inexact body of knowledge. Moreover, less is known about age and growth at the high end. Combine this with the young-of-the-year index, though, and it is possible to predict the size opportunities of striper fishing for a given year.

No accurate, scientific studies predict available 60-pounders, but from memory, my educated guess would be that less than 10 percent of all bass over 50 pounds exceed 60. It gets much worse. Seventy-pounders are not counted in percentages but in years; a generation ago there were three 70-pounders in 15 years, and there had not been any such fish for 54 years before that. Stripers over 80

FORK LENGTH (inches)	WEIGHT (pounds)	AGE (years)
12	½	2
16	1½	3
18–20	2½	4
21–22	4	5
23–25	5	6
27	6½	7
29–32	9	8
34	15	9
38	18	10–12
40–48	28–45	14+
47	42+	16+
49	45–50	18+
50–52	49+	18+

pounds—actually over 125 pounds—have been recorded but never on rod and reel.

Many believe that an all-tackle world record or something close to that in size will produce independent wealth or launch that angler into a new career in outdoor retailing, guiding, or endorsements. I was friendly with Charley Cinto, who boated the biggest lineside in over 50 years, and all he got were two reels, a case of plugs, and a week (without pay) at a sporting show. The notion is somewhat controversial, but I believe that no grand accolades are likely to come to a person who lands a high-level trophy striper. And the idea of overblown rewards has put a price on the head of all important gamefish. What a bounty on a great fish of any species does is act as an incentive for a greater number of cheaters to get involved. It may be important to avoid the appearance of evil as well as the evil itself.

Here are some things that you have to know to prevent yourself from screwing it all up when you do take a monster.

People with a big fish commonly forage around looking for a tackle shop that will give them the best weight. The guy has a 100-pounder but, no, it has to be a 102-pounder. Whenever this is done, it is certain that word of the weight is going to get around; then every ginmill and coffee shop in the state will be abuzz with the results of that weigh station. People know that some weighmasters use a scale on which enough marlin, tuna, and halibut have hanged for 30 years that it reads 6 pounds before anything hangs on it. You could have the next world record, but if some folks saw 98 pounds and others 105, the discrepancy is what they are going to remember. Big-fish news travels fast on the striper coast. Weigh your fish once at a place that is above scrutiny.

CANNIBALISM?

Some people are also concerned these days about stripers being found with juvenile stripers in their stomachs. The logic, which is an extension of human morality, is that the striped bass is so noble a species it would *never* eat its own. Wrong. Stripers, as well as most other species, will eat their young. They always have. It may simply be happening more often now because more small fish are around.

Back when the world was young, I used to be in a fishing contest that required a lineside to weigh 15 pounds even to qualify for competition. One pound less than that, 1 ounce less than that, was worth zilch. After a weekend at the beach I headed home, palms all sweaty, hoping that I could hang the scalp of this striper from my surf belt. I stopped at a tackle shop for a weight and was informed that my bass barely made the eligible weight of 15 pounds. I had a signed and stamped affidavit to prove it.

Then I stopped at the nearby fish market to sell it and was distressed to learn that my fish weighed a mere 13. To me the market clearly had a crooked scale. I was actually ready to call the cops until I realized that tackle shops liked it when you stopped by. What do they care what a fish really weighs as long as they don't have to buy it? The man with the sealed scale, suitable for trade, not fishing contests, even told me that the season was a particularly bad one for 13-pounders, as he had experienced a continuous stream of outraged competitors.

Everybody knows that fish lose weight out of the water. There has been some amateur science in this regard, and the people who have sought to determine a rate of dehydration commonly agree at ½ to 1 percent in a day. However, what I have seen as accepted form is to weigh the fish as soon as possible and make no allowances for dehydration. Still, I have known people to store their huge bass in a bathtub (their wives must love that). Others put the fish under a wet towel in a bed of ice until a shop opens; by the way, this technique is accepted in sport-fishing circles. Garden hoses down the throat are something else.

The issue of weight loss over time gets plenty of attention because sometimes, especially in years when there are concentrations of certain-size fish, coupled with competition, an ounce here or there can make the difference. It is something that people feel they can do something about. At one bluefish tournament in Rhode Island, where the contestants were lined up with their best fish, the sameness of entries became uncanny. The weighmaster was about bored to tears: "Sixteen pounds, two ounces." "Fifteen, fifteen." "Sixteen, one." It seemed that hundreds of blues came from the same mold. Of course the anglers standing in line in the sun were getting nervous, because they truly believed that their weights were melting away. All of a sudden a bluefish exactly the same size as all the others dropped onto the scale and the weighmaster called, "Seventeen, one!" The crowd burst into enthusiastic and simultaneous applause while the proud angler, from Massachusetts I think, blushed with delight. Then the gurry master pressed an ice pick into the fish's gut and a geyser of water rose 5 feet before being blown onto the gallery of onlookers. How this bluefish became pressurized—garden hose or high-speed tow—was never determined, since the champ melted into the crowd.

Because I lived on the beach, my club bought me a good scale, had it sealed, then made me a weighmaster. Once the word got around the beaches that I was an official weighmaster, I noticed two things: My time was no longer my own because of all the surfmen who came to my buggy to weigh their stripers, sometimes after I had gone back to bed; and I was first to learn who was catching what and where. That's another thing about bragging that I should have told you a long time ago. If you are going to show off and boast about all the fish you catch, tell the truth about where you catch them. If there is one thing that others will never forgive you for, it is sending them on a pointless world tour. An old story circulates on the striper coast about the gang being sent to a fictitious spot only to knock them dead there. Surely if striper fishing had its own book of priest and rabbi jokes, the one about a guy showing off a great fish, lying about where it was caught, then having the gang make a killing there would be in it. There is major power in being a weighmaster. In addition to having a little rubber stamp that says so, you have the authority to validate. I once had a guy who wanted an affidavit for a 25-pounder—without the fish—for a bet that he had with a friend. He offered me a case of beer for my trouble.

Shenanigans in the weighing of fish is a direct result of peer pressure, and the worst source of that is competitive fishing. In fact there is little relationship between winning a fishing contest and fishing ability. In early middle age, say 35, I devoted myself to such competition and today view it as one of the darkest periods in my angling life. People who produce contests today have learned to make them less of a slaughter by encouraging catch and release to some degree. They are also smart enough to weigh all fish on the same scale. Even so, some aspects of the results cannot be changed. For instance, it is highly unlikely that the biggest fish will survive. Since no one knows

IGFA Men's Line-Class World Records

Line Class	Weight	Catch Place	Catch Date	Angler
2 lb	21 lb	San Francisco Bay, CA	1/20/92	Kirk E. Campbell
4 lb	40 lb 8 oz	Cape Cod Bay, MA	5/25/85	Christopher Van Duzer
6 lb	56 lb 14 oz	Gay Head, MA	10/15/81	Richard C. Landon
8 lb	41 lb 8 oz	Fisher's Island, NY	8/27/95	Alan Golinski
12 lb	66 lb 12 oz	Bradley Beach, NJ	11/1/79	Steven R. Thomas
16 lb	69 lb	Sandy Hook, NJ	11/18/82	Thomas James Russell
20 lb	78 lb 8 oz	Atlantic City, NJ	9/21/82	Albert R. McReynolds
30 lb	71 lb	Norwalk, CT	7/14/80	John Baldino
50 lb	76 lb	Montauk, L.I., NY	7/17/81	Robert A. Rocchetta
80 lb	70 lb	Orient Point, NY	9/5/87	Chester A. Berry

(Courtesy: International Game Fish Association)

IGFA Women's Line-Class World Records

Line Class	Weight	Catch Place	Catch Date	Angler
2 lb	9 lb 10 oz	Cape Cod Bay, MA	6/7/86	Sharyn Guggino
4 lb	30 lb 6 oz	Cape Cod Bay, MA	5/24/85	Sharyn Guggino
6 lb	46 lb 12 oz	Fisher's Island, NY	9/4/95	Emme Golinski
8 lb	40 lb 2 oz	Millicoma River, OR	4/5/85	Edna Skinner
12 lb	48 lb 9 oz	Deal, NJ	7/27/80	Edna Yates
16 lb	48 lb 8 oz	Monomoy Island, MA	7/16/91	Connie Codner
20 lb	57 lb 8 oz	Block Island Sound, NY	8/28/59	Mary R. Aubry
30 lb	64 lb 8 oz	North Truro, MA	8/14/60	Rosa O. Webb
50 lb	64 lb	Sea Bright, NJ	6/27/71	Mrs. Asie Espenak
80 lb	57 lb 4 oz	Watch Hill, RI	8/24/97	Janice Masciarelli

(Courtesy: International Game Fish Association)

which fish is going to win, you usually see killed any number of big fish that fall just short of the winning position. Saltwater striper tournaments also have a problem that seems to defy solution—the difference between a surf winner, a boat winner, and an overall winner. It is widely known that fishing from shore is unlikely to produce the overall winner, given the usual disparity in results between surf and boat fishing. Now, it's not the top fish that's the problem, but how it is registered. For instance, let's say "Buck" has a 40-pound bass for the tourney but has just learned that a 42 is in the lead. And Buck is registered in the boat division, so he can't submit it in the surf division. But Buck knows that his 40 will win from shore, so he gives it to his brother-in-law, "Dinkie," who is registered in the surf. Tournament officials had hoped to prevent this through a registration process that forced all to declare how they were going to fish. Where was Dinkie fishing all this time? In the boat with Buck, who would bring in any fish that *either* of them caught depending upon which category suited what they got. As a surfcaster, I will never enter another contest, because officials cannot offer a suitable prize for shore fishers. If they do, it will only encourage more cheating. I once actually won the shore part of a tourney with a 38-pounder that paid off in a lawn mower worth under $100. Meanwhile, the winner of the overall contest—a boat fish in the high 50s—took home over $5,000 in prizes. Not bad nearly 30 years ago.

The late Gene Lambert, a competent striper fisherman whom I knew for over a generation, once brought a 52-pounder to a tourney in which he was registered. All contest fish were placed in a cooler for sale later. Within a day Gene's monster slipped into second place. Asking to see the new lead striper, Gene was shown his own fish. Pointing this out, he was told that *his* fish had been sold so that it would be fresh for the market. Who caught the new lead fish in the contest that no one got to see? A member of the club that was running the contest. Hello, are you still there?

TWO

The Politics of Striper Management

THE INTERRELATIONSHIP among brood stock, spawning river, and the resultant fecundity is basic to the continuance of the striped bass fishery. The striper coast can harbor no trophy stripers without concern for its small fish. There can be no juveniles without care for the breeding stock. Reproductive success begins in the rivers, the very womb of the striper nursery. How this is accomplished is what sparks contention among amateurs and professionals, betwixt northerners and southerners, between sport and commercial interests.

There exists today, much as it has since my first cast nearly 50 years ago, the simplistic notion that all we need to do to preserve striped bass are *never* to kill a fish and to stop pollution. This is supposed to be done by instituting a no-sell law for commercial anglers and mandatory catch and release for us. We could initiate a few thousand laws, as has been done with guns, public health, and child care,

Management—which gave us trophy stripers—began with protecting our "schoolies." Maybe we've learned to care for the resource.

and all feel better because we would have done something. But before anything is done, a causal relationship should be established between what we do and what is perceived as wrong with striper management. What keeps preventing us from shaping striper management to sport fishing's concerns alone are the complexities related to traditional use, the satisfaction of both commercial and sport-fishing interests, and consumer access to stripers as a source of protein. Much as I wish they did, stripers do not belong to sport fishing.

The first obstacle to be overcome is the establishment of regulations within the sport-fishing community that will contribute to striper conservation. To a great degree this has been done already: Conservative size limits were established during the striper moratorium of the 1980s. A problem with size limits, like other regulations, is that they lack uniformity; they vary from state to state. This has caused a great deal of distress, because it is puzzling to release a bass in Connecticut that would be legal in Rhode Island and taken commercially from Massachusetts to be sold in New York. Keep in mind that, while many states now have no-sell laws, some allow commercial fishing, whether with nets or rod and reel (as is the case in Massachusetts).

I realize that one solution would be banning the sale of bass by raising size limits high enough so that most stripers would enjoy release. This happened during the moratorium in the 1980s and found its most extreme application in the 1990s.

But the problem with this can be illustrated by the story of how the forthcoming year's regulations were once formulated. One state lowered its size limit to 34 inches. Distressed by this, officials of a striper group said that no member would be allowed to kill a bass under 36. Not wanting to be outdone, a charter skipper in the same area said that no fish under 40 inches would be killed on his boat. I don't know how far this one-up contest to determine who most loved stripers really went. The point is, does such behavior spring from a genuine concern to protect stripers from overexploitation, or are the politically correct notions of our time simply a way to get elected to a chair or to engage more charters? It is a great example, however, of what can happen when amateurs seek to manage wildlife. They don't manage stripers; rather, they seek to show the public at large—who either elect them or purchase their services (or their books)—that they love the bass the most.

Moratorium protection for the 1982 Maryland year-class was ratcheted upward to stay ahead of growth. This is why anglers from the mid-1980s saw size limits climb from the traditional 16-inch minimum to as large as 36 inches. There was good reason for this: The fishery's last hope was pinned to this moderate, albeit best in its time, year-class with an index of 8. Noble as the effort may have been, it failed to take the realities of what had been made a harvestable fish into account. With so many new striper fishers on the scene, people were fishing in a sea where it was nearly impossible to find a keeper. Their best tease was a bass that was barely under the legal size limit. Try to imagine the frustration you might experience from beaching or boating a bass that was just short of 3 feet long, weighed 18 pounds, and had to be released because it was too small. A sociological truth tells us that conformity to law begins with agreement; so do you see something unrealistic in this picture? I am aware that there are some people around who could release 18-pounders without a whimper: those who caught them when they were last around, or who do not eat fish, or—in spite of never coming home with a fish—whose spouses believe that they were really fishing.

We are a culture in transition when it comes to consuming fish. I have witnessed a generation of anglers come along behind me who are embarrassed and horrified at the notion of killing anything. They view hunting as murder. But then they order filet mignon or veal for dinner. They release stripers then purchase cod, which are on the verge of commercial extinction. Some of the most vocal protectors of striped bass will stand or drift in a tiderip that is visibly shaded with the forms of countless linesides, all too small to keep, and release dozens if not hundreds of them. Yet study upon study tells us that from 8 to 24 percent of returned bass (depending on the method) will die from having been caught and released. Who does more harm to a fishery: the person who kills 2 and takes them home for t or the one who releases 50 to have 4 die and be wasted? Catch and release gets a bad name when people won't leave small fish alone.

Many release regulations, while popular in some quarters, remain unworkable in the context of varied use and cultural diversity. Today's striper fishers often come from backgrounds where no-kill is a way of life. Others, now a minority, view hauling a little Atlantic protein for personal use a birthright. There ought to be room for both. Nonetheless, some regulations regarding size restrictions and bag limits are needed.

In my youth I saw people come from Maine with coolers filled with graying landlocked salmon and monster brook trout. In the 1980s I saw Atlantic salmon fishers limit themselves to 1 wild fish per day and still legally kill 30 per year, a number way beyond consumption levels and one that helped spawn the conservative measures in place today. Not only are past abuses well documented, but there are many who still recall them; our more youthful brethren need only ask around if they doubt such things took place. Still, this is not an issue of politics or viewpoint, it is one of professional management—doing what is good for a fishery based upon science. For instance, a Massachusetts reservoir overpopulated with lake trout in 1997 was determined by project biologists to need from 2 to 3,000 pounds of lakers harvested in order to protect the forage base. Their concerns were born from watching declining growth rates of what had formerly been healthy lakers, as well as from samples of a plummeting population of smelt (the prime food of the lake trout). It took officials years to raise the kill rate, because of the universal belief that it was bad for the fishery to kill any trout. Indeed, the no-kill ethic so dominated attitudes that managers determined only 50 percent of participating anglers killed any fish at all—even when urged to do so by the Fisheries and Wildlife Department. Lake trout are simply delicious, yet consumption remains an unacceptable alternative for many of us. This says something about naive notions regarding fish-

While fighting a striper, this surfcaster is trying to decide if it is right to keep it.

eries management. There are people who believe that if we stop killing fish, we will forever enjoy utopian angling.

I am not urging a reversal of the no-kill ethic here. Indeed, what I have seen since I was old enough to observe fish shows me that wise use has become the salvation of sport fishing. Still, it is foolish to believe that all we need is protection. For example, a riverine environment that precludes spawning due to its adverse conditions, natural or man-made, shuts down recruitment. What man does later with the fish is not relevant if the fish are not born. It becomes immaterial whether suitable regulations were in place to protect the brood stock. As a culture in transition regarding protein utilization, if regulations are unrealistic there will be no conformity with regard to killing. People will take what they need, just as they go 40 miles per hour in a 25 zone if the speed limit lacks good sense. Conformity begins with agreement. Yet if a suitable replacement protein were available that destroyed all our incentive to kill wild striped bass, we would see an end both to sport fishermen taking home their legal limit—in some cases two 30-pounders that produce fresh fillets for 40 people—and to commercial netters encircling an entire school, stacking the legal ones like cordwood, and allowing the already dead sublegals to rot with the bergalls.

I believe the answer lies in sportsmen applying a higher ethic when they choose their fishing method. Multitreble hooks inflict many small injuries that slow hook removal and increase the danger of the fish suffocating. Moreover, have you ever backed a hook from the eyeball of a fish and wondered what its chances were of seeing again out of that eye? Single-hook artificials, like jigs and flies, often inflict a single, high-penetration injury, especially upon small fish— which are the ones most likely to be returned. Barbless hooks, while popular and considered favorable to survival, penetrate as well as those with barbs. A widespread custom in bait fishing is to pin a chunk of forage species to a treble hook. Some barbs will retain this bait, and all are capable of hooking the fish. Usually the quarry (probably but not necessarily a striper) is permitted to take, or swallow, the bait; the fish is then hooked deep in the gut or the gullet opening at the bottom of the throat. Fish are rarely lost when hooked this way, but I suspect that the method is responsible for a dramatic reduction in their survival rate. It takes too long to remove such a hook, and too much injury is inflicted upon vital organs. Clipping the leader quickly is an option if the hook is not stainless, but I still have doubts about the future of any fish with a treble lodged in its throat. Any angler with a moderate level of experience has seen fish with single hooks in their paunch at various stages of decomposition. Haven't you? As bad as the prognosis might be for a gut-hooked fish, though, a surprising number of mouth-hooked fish do survive. How bad is it, then?

The following nonstriper examples are useful because they took place in a controlled environment, where the results of release could be observed more easily than in a boundless sea. I've spent many weeks in winter on a steelhead river, where hundreds of anglers using artificials released thousands of fish, and found only an occasional steelhead washed up. In a private trout club, where hundreds of trout were stocked regularly and dozens of members spent uncountable hours catching and releasing them, a dead trout lying on the bottom is rare. And in catch-and-release public waters it is unusual to see a dead trout. It could be that the anglers represented in these examples have experience, know that speed in bringing fish in is a factor, and most likely fly fish, a method universally believed to inflict the least angling mortality. Another factor that influences fatality is water temperature: Cold water is thought to minimize development of lactic acid. Of course, any injury to the gills, which bleed easily, is widely thought to spell curtains for the fish.

Overall I think barbless hooks increase any fish's chance for survival, but if they are easier to remove for us, they are also easier for the fish to remove when it is on the end of your line. Much of the time you will know something of the potential of the angling situation in which you are involved; that means you should use an easy-release hook much of the time. Conversely, if I were to encounter the next world record, I would hope that what's been included in fish-hook design since the Pleistocene—the barb—would be there.

A growing number of consumer states are passing laws against the use of gaffs for landing fish. It escapes me, but the apparent logic

is that too many people have been seen holding fish up for measurement with gaffs, judging the catch short, then releasing the fish.
Certainly such behavior makes no sense. In a half century of fishing,
however, I have never seen this done. And—think about it—a gaff is
not needed for a fish too small to keep. The issue of protecting small
fish with antigaffing laws has no relevance. What does need protection is our right to gaff an outsize striper. There are many situations
where the use of a gaff is not simply a convenience, it is imperative.
In open-sea fishing on jetties or on rocky shores where anglers are
elevated, a long-handled gaff is an absolute necessity. It is also needed in bridge fishing, or on high docks, or when wading the flats long
distances from shore and dealing with a fish you want to keep. Gaffs
are silly for 10-pound fish, but how else would you subdue a 50- or
60-pounder alongside your boat? There is no management relevance
in the issue of whether or not you use a gaff. What is pertinent is
whether or not you kill a fish. As long as killing is going to be allowed,
it is not just pointless to ban gaff use, it is patently stupid to make
the act of catching and keeping less efficient. Indeed such regulations are symptomatic of a greater malaise: the need to demonstrate
a commitment to management more for its own sake than for any
true result.

Since the dawn of wildlife management, it has been the custom
in our culture to protect small fish in favor of harvesting the larger
ones. Presented in their worst form, size limits have been set too
close to the fish that regulations were intended to protect. Thus, a
minority of those individual fish that exhibited an unanticipated rate
of growth actually were large enough to keep and became a target in
sport fishing. In this way we have unwittingly removed from the gene
pool the very striped bass that exhibited a propensity for favorable
growth. The late Lee Wulff, whose writing and contributions to sport
fishing with the fly have endeared him to millions, lamented for
much of his life, "What farmer would slaughter his finest brood stock

25

and keep his runts?" The sentiment of giving small fish a chance at existence is simply an anthropomorphic notion about the value of life plugged into our protein supply. We need a better grip on which fish should be allowed to be harvested and which should be permitted to continue to contribute to a more refined gene pool in perpetuation of the species. They are reservoirs of fecundity. If conditions are right, relatively few females can produce a lot of young. Our cows, our breeders, should live. The small fish, half of which are males whose function can easily be assumed by others, should be made available to the consumer if there is going to be any kill at all.

I am aware that there is strong movement afoot to preserve all striped bass. How that is to be accomplished is a never-ending exercise in management by consensus. As far back as 40 years ago, people quarreled about the release of stripers. Such disagreement is, in part, why most states end up with different regulations than their neighbors. At any rate, here is my take on it: The protection of breeders is what is needed. Contrary to popular belief, these producer fish—which can be fertilized by small males—are not the monster bass this book is about; they are largely the 15- to 40-pounders. The 50- and 60-pounders no longer contribute or, if they do, represent a tiny minority of the brood stock. What should be allowed is the harvest of some small fish, half of which are males, along with the truly large ones, all of which are females. The ones in between—from say 15 to 40 pounds, and all females by virtue of their size—are in need of protection. Maine was the first striper consumer state to do this. Slot limits, which should be the same for all states because all states are drawing from the same population of northwestern Atlantic stripers, would fill this need to some degree. However, slot limits, which permit the taking of fish between certain sizes, are controversial because this is rocket science for some people.

I'm confounded by the inception of striper seasons—especially in places that, due to geography, already suffer from a short season.

Slot-limit stripers. Will this be the answer to determining how we apportion our catch?

It is a pity to me that after enduring a moratorium that saw not only no striper fishing but even little *writing* about it, the people who fish there cannot take full advantage of the bass restoration that has at long last come to pass. Again, if continued restoration efforts are no longer a problem, why are solutions still in place from a time we would all just as soon forget? Stripers are restored, but we insist upon trembling at the notion that we might lose them again.

The more complicated the regulation is, the more likely it is to become an issue that begs for a higher level of enforcement. In my time at the shore, I have met just one conservation officer, and he was entirely out of his element. Most jurisdictions of the striper coast are sadly wanting in enforcement and, invariably, we will hear a call to do something. The reasoning is bound to beg the issue of financing enforcement, and the answer will be the establishment of a saltwater license. Which sounds great on paper—but then, so does a rosier, more promising, more imposing government. I oppose the imposition of a saltwater license, because it would once again be a solution unrelated to the problem, if there is, at this writing, any problem at all.

Increasingly, marine biologists are expressing concern with biobalance. In the case of stripers, they may be doing more predation than the forage base can sustain. Whispered remarks that "We could do with a few less stripers" give rise to a second concern: How best to tell an often hostile public—who can never have enough bass—that the ecosystem is maxed out? Massachusetts Marine Fisheries, much to the distress of a growing number of striper organizations, has sought to put stripers on the tables of those who do not fish, to manage and market bass in a controlled way. But the striper-watch crowd rails at the idea of seeing a bass in the display case of any fish market. One side worries about having enough linesides to eat and develop, and the other side fears and distrusts government. Modern fisheries management first saw this controversy with Great Lakes salmonids, which were believed to have been overstocked. Our striper restoration may have resulted in a similar situation—more stripers than can grow well on the striper coast. Just to throw my iron in the fire, I think that overforaging by stripers is not likely to be a problem because of the decline in bluefish, pollack, and cod. Still, who really knows?

If 20 years of talking to striper-fishing audiences has taught me anything, it is that they find the subject of bass management frustrating and offensive. (I had the same feeling writing this chapter.) Distrusting government, they have grown weary of managers' solutions as well as of much of what is offered on their side. I vacillate

For too long we have hounded the poor fish to the point where we would happily slug it out to determine who makes the last cast for the very last striped bass.

between the two sides—while also haunted by a back-of-the-mind suspicion that it is all bull in the rushes; the bass are going to go their own way in spite of us. I recall when we killed a fish and felt good about making certain that it was a scant 16 inches. We thought that market fishing with a "pole"—sometimes even a fly rod—was a noble endeavor. How things change. Still, I cannot say with any certainty that we were so wrong, because we may not even have been actors in the play. Sometimes, when I feel the sibilance of the shore in the bottoms of my boots, there is a sense of frailty, a sense of desperation in my efforts to understand more. Most of all I fear those who have all the answers; it is they, it seems, who know the least.

The entire point of striper management, or at least the part that boils in controversy, is that too many fish are killed. It matters little who harvests them—a small number of efficient commercial anglers or a much larger group of highly limited sport fishers. (The combined effect of the latter is greater than the kill of netters, haul seiners, and trap operators.) What if incentives for taking linesides were rendered ineffectual, the price removed from the fish's head? What if, like salmon, a striper product could be produced commercially that cost less and could be marketed with little fluctuation in price while remaining socially and environmentally acceptable? Raising protein from the sea, similar to what we learned long ago when we moved from hunting to animal husbandry, is the next step in the road. We presently raise shrimp, shellfish, catfish, and salmon, to name only some. However, the best model is the salmon, for which high-seas fishing is now less practical. Even sport fishers release a wild salmon, buy a fillet from commercial aquaculture, then raise their glass to the best of both worlds. Similarly, farming of domestic stripers or hybrids would make available a market bass and remove incentive for killing wild fish. Effective research is already being carried out to develop a suitable striper or striper hybrid toward that end. Much like the chicken industry, they are now trying to squeeze a little more effi-ciency out of the beasts. While it is too early to say if developments are in the offing that will emasculate commercial activity and reduce angling mortality, aquaculture is such a rapidly developing science that I think it only a matter of time. At this writing striper aquacul-ture production has enjoyed a 600 percent growth in five years. Is that Twilight Zone music I hear in the background? Try this strongly related notion.

Advances in DNA technology have made stock identification an accurate science. It is now possible to identify the river of origin of any striper. Let's suppose for a moment that we find in the future a "family" of stripers exhibiting a greater potential for growth than usual. Isolation of breeds that exhibit a certain trait—intelligence, rapid growth, or morphology—has been done with mammals for cen-turies. It was not done sooner with fish because isolation of genetics was difficult with wild breeds in a nonhuman environment. Let us suppose further that upon examination of these huge stripers a DNA match keeps showing up that leads us to accurately identify these unique giants as a particular identifiable group from which we can accurately and reliably draw. Certainly selective breeding is nothing new. Farmers and hunters have known for centuries that genetic propensity could be bred in while certain undesirable traits or characteristics could be avoided. Thus, it is not outside the bounds of logic that a superpopulation or strain of striper could be first isolated, then cultivated for stocking. Propagation and stocking are old sciences; it is the application of DNA knowledge toward the goals of bigger bass that is new. Imagine a sea with little harvest of a fish that was genetically engineered to grow larger.

Still, never forget that nature has fine-tuned the bass's growth rate to its environment. Let's move back to thicker ice.

There is some controversy over the practice of mounting game-fish. One view is that a dead bass is not a bass. As with many contemporary notions, I disagree. It is only natural, particularly in view of how much is often required to catch such a fish, to want it for posterity. The feeling of sitting in the comfort of your own space and looking at a dream fish on your wall is something that offers a great deal of enjoyment; it gives more to any species than it takes away. If more people could look upon a great fish that they could call their own, they would be less inclined to continue killing them. I benefited from this experience both in trout fishing and surfcasting. Once I could look up at a mount, it meant less to me to kill more fish. Still, it was no less exciting for me to shake the hook from a 5-pound trout or a 40-pound striper just because there was always a better one looking down at me in my home.

Once this is an option, two methods of taxidermy need examination: the traditional skin mount (stuffing the actual fish) and the marine method (using the fish as a pattern for a casting). In the skin mount, biodegradation over the years often causes cracking and discoloration. It might take 10 or 20 years, but skin mounts do lose color and perfection. They are, however, the real fish, which has always been the greatest selling point for the method. Marine mounts, or replicas, are not the fish; a mold is poured around the original. Usually separated around a parting line after they dry, the two halves of the mold are in negative form. It is like printing your foot in mud or plaster: You end up with a perfect negative replica of the shoe, exact in size and shape. It is then possible to reproduce that shoe in positive form with a light, strong, resistant material and to paint or color it appropriately. So it is with a marine-mounted fish casting. Because the new "fish" is of hollow, light fiberglass, it will always look the same.

With the marine method, the technology used could reproduce one fish an almost unlimited number of times. It would take but one 50-pounder, or one of every size on either side of that, to replicate the fish that the angler sought to "preserve." Such counterfeits would mean we'd kill no more than 1 fish for more than 100, if not 1,000, but still enjoy all the pleasures of having a mount. Comfortable attitudes could be fostered about having, enjoying, boasting about our success—without consumption. This would in the long run save the mightiest of stripers.

Nothing said here is meant to steer management, set policy, define conservation dogma, or change ethics. There are too many issues before us for agreement to present itself on all of them. And among nonprofessional anglers, much of this stuff is passed on from father to son; when you try to change perceptions, you're doing so not only with individuals but against the resiliency of generations.

Three

Losing the Best Ones

ALL THROUGH the postmoratorium period, when the world of striper fishing was reemerging, I fielded questions from anxious surfcasters about the availability of keepers. I was talking to hundreds of fishers at the many seminars that I conduct about fishing for bass. The universal frustration was that these people were, in many cases, catching hundreds of fish each season but couldn't get any large enough to keep. Invariably I would question them about their experiences striper fishing, and more often than not, when asked if they had lost any decent fish, the answer would be—after some hesitation, some embarrassment—that they had.

Two things were probably responsible for the loss of the more important fish: The hook pulled out, or the line broke. Most often, especially with really big bass, losses were attributable to the latter. These exchanges on the subject became so characteristic that I soon learned to do my questioning in private; it was too embarrassing to have the discussion in front of an audience. Naturally my answer was that

WHY WE LOSE THE BEST ONES
1. Fishing too light—break-offs.
2. Poor equipment maintenance—especially lines.
3. No suitable landing contingencies.
4. Allowing a slack line.
5. Inexperience.
6. Pulling too hard.
7. Panic.
8. Running out of line.
9. Crowds.
10. Hurrying while fighting a fish.

only the bigger bass tax a line to its breaking point. True, it was a generalization, but it probably did explain the loss in most situations. I was not there, but I've been there often enough for my own fish to know that losses increase with bigger fish. Because they lack experience, many anglers don't know the breaking limits of their equipment. You can only pull so hard on a big fish before the line snaps. Worse, many breaks occur because the fish happens to pull very hard at the same time you do; then there are two sources of overt strain with which the tackle must contend. Never forget that it is not the rod or the reel that is going to burst, it's the line. The line is your parachute.

Inevitably, after we had so many small fish for so many years, our equipment choices evolved downward. It is only natural, if you've caught 200 schoolies in a given season, to tailor what you use to what you're catching. The logic is that you don't hunt squirrels with an AK-47. Moreover, light tackle is more user-friendly because it is lightweight while producing greater casting distances with less effort. And the lighter lures we use with light equipment lead to more hits. Freshwater tackle in the salt delivers lures that are often close in size to the forage and fit in the mouth of even a bucketmouth striper. For generations outdoor magazines have advanced the notion that the use of light tackle is more sporting, that it is the choice of pros. In fact the reverse is true. Pros fish right, and hunting bear with a .22 is wrong. Even a fisher who is experienced enough to take on a huge

Because they lack experience, many anglers don't know the breaking limits of their equipment. You can only pull so hard on a big fish before the line breaks.

striper with kids' equipment faces practically insurmountable obstacles to putting such a fish on the beach.

Fishing commercially 30 years ago, while raising four children on Cape Cod beaches, we had dozens of experiences of monster fish overwhelming what we used. Keep in mind that all of us, even the youngest of the three girls, had extensive backgrounds in the striper

People learn to handle fish through experience with small ones. Then a big striper, a trophy striper, comes along and the line is broken.

surf and had caught hundreds of two-handed stripers. Still the temptation to reach for that little "schoolie rod" was so universal that all four of our youngsters quarreled over it; they eventually agreed to take turns with it. Invariably one of them would fetch Dad, because the child exercising his or her turn was on to a trophy striper. Typically I would find the child following downtide, the drag humming. The most productive way to assess the situation was to look at how much of the reel's capacity remained. Of course, in a balanced outfit, the capacity of the reel in yards was about what we were all used to with the proper-weight tackle—over 240 yards. It was the size of the line, its volume, its strength, that were wanting. With light line, effective fishing requires a light drag. The striper runs a greater distance from you more easily; in minutes all the line is out there, with little remaining on the reel. Worse, the fish—and I'm not talking a routine, everyday fish here—is not tired from its efforts. You are low on line and fighting a green fish.

Strong gamefish, green fish, have their "head." What this means is that the fish is able to freely turn its head in any direction. (It's opposed to a situation in which a fisher with heavy tackle keeps moving the fish toward the beach, where its head is facing the surfcaster. Fish cannot swim backward.) You can tell that a big fish has its head if you feel blows to the taut line. It is as though someone is striking your line with a stick, and it provides clear evidence that you are feeling each pump of the striper's tail as it seeks to swim off. A fish with its head can breathe more comfortably and change direction with ease, and trouble often comes with those changes of direction. There are two reasons: First, the hook can pull free from a *new* force direction; second, a free-swimming fish will inevitably wrap a turn of line around its body. Trouble.

One night in Charlestown, Rhode Island, I was standing with our daughter Sandra while she fought on light tackle a monster that happened to be mixed with a bunch of small bass. After close to an hour of trading back and forth, I watched her line go slack. She had done nothing wrong. There were no overt forces applied. Still, the line had failed. I don't say broken, because what really happened was the last 5 feet of line was laced with little nicks and cuts from having worked itself under the silver-dollar-size scales of the moby bass. And with each pump of its body, each flexing, some parts of the line were run across those scales, and some parts were moved under new scales. Thus, we not only had weak sections, we had multiple sections of damaged line. The 12-pound-test line was reduced to 4. While this is not a book about children, I can tell you that they cry when dream fish break free . . . just like their parents.

Some people think that a solution to line damaged from wrapping the body lies in adding a heavy section or "shocker" at the leader end. That would only be the answer if the connection between the running line and the leader were yielding 100 percent knot strength. True, you might be better than I at making a suitable connection between line and heavy shocker, but how strong would it be after hitting the guides a few hundred times? Having seen such shockers tied on 50-pound-class surf tackle fail many times, I would not resort to a shocker tying 50-pound mono to 50-pound braid. You ought to see the astonishment that I've witnessed from experienced surfcasters when they broke off a cow flailing in the last wave and found their shocker was gone—clear evidence that the knot failed. Do you know anyone who has ever taken a line, leader, shocker, and terminal and pulled on it with a measuring device to determine the rig's breaking strength? We all should. Another thing that I like to do is the simple test of hooking up to the bumper of my buggy or back fence and pulling as hard as I would dare with a fish. While it evaluates for failure, it also gives me confidence in what I'm doing.

Bluefish are less of a problem these days, but they could well increase again in the future, and they can also raise holy hell with a good line. You've likely been into a school of blues, perhaps fighting one, when everything suddenly went slack because a blue saw a weed jiggle on your line, struck it, and cut you off. Only what if such a marauder struck a weed, damaged the line, and swam off? You, without the slightest inclination, are now fishing half a line. Before a night of fishing begins, stretch out your line a cast's worth and run your fingers over it. Knowing the breaking strength of your equipment is basic tackle management. 'Chutes that don't open are the fault of the packer: you.

The greatest damage to line comes from the cast, and this is going to happen at the point where the line is in contact with the tip when you drop trailing distance from tip to casting weight. The heavier the casting weight, the fewer casts should be allowed before that line is removed. *Cutting back,* a term used by competent surfcasters for removing the last 3 or more feet of line, is a way of freshening the most active portion of a fishing line. This renders something close to full line strength, and fresh knots are likely stronger than old ones. Not only should lines be cut back after a few hours of casting, they should be cut back more often during blitz conditions if fish of any size are being hooked regularly.

Our sport is rife with trade-offs. It is easier to fish with light tackle, but the fish that we would like to catch with this equipment often overwhelm it. Thus, a perfect world would offer us 10-pound-test performance while yielding 100 pounds of strength. Let

IT'S THE KNOT, STUPID

You'll hear a lot of people blame the loss of a trophy striper squarely upon the shoulders of a wild beast that was merely trying to get away: "It broke my line." Wrong. *It did not break your line. You broke your knot.* Unless they are damaged, lines rarely break; knots do. Moreover, if a line does break, then it is because of a well-tied knot.

Knots are important because by their very nature, they tend to damage line when tied. It is thus incumbent upon the fisher to produce a knot as close as possible to the rated strength of his line. Good knots are generally 90 percent of line strength or better; thus, 20-pound line will fail at the knot at 18 pounds of pull. Things you can do to achieve such ratings include tying carefully according to a knot's specifications, and lubricating the knot with saliva while cinching it up. I tie everything with a clinch knot accompanied by a single overhand knot outside, so that if it slips it will stop at the overhand. If you check my shoelaces, you'll understand why I don't write books about knots and why I usually avoid the subject.

Years ago, after a bunch of the guys had lost some moby bass in the surf—right where we usually pressure them, in the last wave—somebody got the idea of using a 20-foot "shock leader" for the last yards of the landing. It sounds good on paper, but in practice they lost even more behemoths because of failure of the knot between the shock leader and the running line. The knot was pounded on the guides each cast, and it often took a chunk of flesh from the caster's thumb on its way past, too. Tying mono to mono damages both, and this was no solution.

Freshwater tackle in the salt? It is easier to fish with light tackle, but the fish we would like to catch with this equipment often overwhelm it.

me repeat: If you make contact with a moby striper, your greatest risk is breaking off. However, contemporary science has made the compromise easier with smaller lines that are less likely to break.

Around 1990 more was done to advance the overall performance of fishing lines than had taken place in probably 30 years. I'm not going to start naming brands and materials, because these change too rapidly to have any value in a lasting treatise. However, I can talk size and strength.

Heavy spinning line is at maximum strength at .019 inch (I'll get to pound test in a minute). If you seek to fish larger than that, spool depletion snubs down the casting distance and capacity is too low. For all the time that I have been fishing, mono of .019 inch (plus or minus) was 20-pound test, but new developments in line—copolymers, for one—now offer that diameter in 30-pound test. What this means is that we can now enjoy the performance qualities of the lighter line we are accustomed to while spinning with 30 pound. You are fishing with your father's line, in other words, but have 50 percent more strength. You have a bear rifle that handles like a squirrel gun.

A similar advance in lines has taken place in conventional or revolving-spool equipment. Again, if you choose mono, then the trade-offs allow for greater strength. With braided line—a product that enjoys less acceptance—the improvements are even more dramatic; it is now possible to cast 60- or even 70-pound line while fishing with the feel of 40. I have broken off with 50 but never fished any larger; it was not practical with the old lines. As our targets grow, casting with 60- and 70-pound line will be both comfortable and utilitarian.

Further contrasting spinning and conventional tackle, spinning tackle dominates angling choices because it is efficient and easy to use. The aforementioned line developments close the gap between spinning and conventional equipment somewhat, but the old revolving-spool gear still enjoys the advantage of offering the greatest strength—roughly twice as much. Still, that stronger choice requires a higher level of expertise. A revolving spool must be wound on the level and usually, but not necessarily, by hand with an "educated thumb" that will have a groove worn into it after only one night of fishing. If this reel is not thumbed—more thumb education—properly during the cast to prevent override of the spool when the cast

Light tackle is user-friendly. But are you bear hunting with a squirrel gun?

slows, it will snarl or backlash hopelessly. The tackle choice of so-called pros is not an easy one but it does deal with many of the obstacles that I've outlined.

The one application of conventional tackle that I have often seen and has always confounded me is fishing lighter lines, say under 20-pound test. Freshwater baitcasting defeats the entire justification for this tackle—its strength. Certainly anyone wanting to enjoy the comforts and pleasures of fishing light should choose to fish light spinning gear. At any rate, light baitcasting is one more option, and variations in equipment are a big part of the fun.

Contrary to what many might believe, fly fishing is *not* light tackle. Properly set up, the weakest link in the fly-fishing chain should be the tippet section of the leader. For the fish I'm talking about here, that would be 20 pound with the old leader materials, or 30 with copolymers. It is mandatory that this tippet section be the weakest link to the spool bottom; otherwise you risk losing fly line through a break in the backing or even in the fly line itself. Again, if you use state-of-the-art lines, an appropriate increase in backing strength can compensate for heavier leaders without loss of suitable spool capacity—200 yards plus. If you've been fishing for stripers for less than 10 years, these are probably all things that you've never cared about. Start.

The risks of having an outlandishly large striper fall from the hook, pull free, or drop are the same as these risks for small fish. We all deal with the unknown quantity of a certain amount of steel, the hook, and whatever penetration that it enjoys into the fish's maw. When that line goes tight from the take, there is no way of knowing how much purchase has occurred between steel and flesh. We can only subdue the fish as best we can, minimizing forces while dealing with all the strength trade-offs. We can also keep a tight line to prevent the hook from backing as a result of changes in direction. I am convinced that far fewer big bass are lost to drops than to break-offs. Nonetheless, you never forget them no matter how they are lost.

Still, I have spent a lifetime watching anglers around me lament drop losses as though the fault were theirs. Maybe it's due to the notion that if keeping a tight line prevents drops, then experiencing a drop must be evidence of allowing slack. It simply is not necessarily so. The best batters will miss the ball regularly. But the pain persists.

Around 30 years ago, while fishing a Rhody beach late in September with a couple of surf buddies, I cast a Creek Chub Giant Pikie Minnow, one of the biggest plugs made, into the daylight surf. True, it was daylight, a time less likely to produce. The surf was up

pretty high, providing cover for any cow that might have been foraging the shore. I fished hard to keep my friends honest and they, sky-
larking, ragged on me as I knocked my brains out. Then, in the first
wave, a fish took down that plug in as hard a take as you are ever going
to get, and I was onto a huge striped bass. Loaded for bear—a squidder with 50-pound braid—I fought the fish only a few minutes,
always snubbing when she sought to swim the side of a foamer.
"Right there!" I shouted, pointing at a green lineside before she was
inundated with suds. One of the guys went down to put a handle on
her, but he came back running from the surf as the curl of sea bulged
over his head. There is always another wave, and he just waited for
another chance to go back down. Of course he kept looking at me,
then out over the first wave. Only this time when he looked back he
saw my expression, my level stick. "No!" he uttered in disbelief. She
was gone. I wanted to cry.

The notion that a fish you lose is outrageously large is not all that
unusual. Over and over we've heard of trophy stripers within our
grasp that escaped at the last possible moment. Years ago a member
of our striper club was fishing live mackerel in his boat where he
could see the linesides cruising in full daylight around the baits. At
first one bass seemed to be playing with the mackerel, but then it
would dart onto the bait and take it down. Bob, a lifelong carpenter
with a good muscular build, fought a 44-pounder to the gunwales and
hauled it over quite effortlessly with one hand. A short while later he
fought one much larger, grasped it by the gills, but could not heave
it over the gunwales. Tiring in the standoff, Bob could see his gaff in
the bow and let go of the bass to go for it. Still in contact with the
brute, as he came aft with the grapple he watched it shake the hook,
pause in the sunlight as if to catch its breath, then sink out of sight
like a very bad dream. Question: If Bob could raise a 44-pounder with
one arm, yet he couldn't bring this one over the side with two, how
big was it? We'll never know.

Big stripers are often lost because of the many adversities we face.

In the early 1990s, when the fish started coming back, George began taking Barbara out onto the beach in Provincetown on Cape Cod. Having fished the area nearly 20 years before, he knew the ropes. For him, however, it was not simply a case of knowing the fishing. You had to know how to survive the beach situation. In this part of the world, where people come from all over, from diverse backgrounds, not all are looking for the same thing. Some are tourists just out for a night of fishing. Others might be rod-and-reel commercial anglers who are masterful at reading a situation. A curious interaction has evolved here: People are always trying to get the drop on one another in terms of where the fish are, what they are taking, who is getting what. As a consequence, George lived in terror of having someone come upon him when he was into a fish. Not that it happened that often. The few times that he had ever beached a decent striper, Barbara had not been with him. But she was always with him when the fishing was bad.

Anyway, one night beneath the flash of one of the lighthouses (we won't say which) they found cows cruising the shallows. First their attention had been drawn to it all by a subtle *plop* as a fish turned to inhale a sand eel. Then another. George's plug was hammered by a fish just as the lighthouse completed a revolution, giving him a chance to see that these were no schoolies. He really never hooked it, but the sound of it throwing water so close to the beach had Barbara's attention. Consequently, she was watching his retrieve while paying little attention to her own—until her plug stopped cold.

"George?" she asked, fully conscious that this was not something with which she had ever been confronted.

"George?"

Under the flash of the lighthouse, this monster threw water for 10 feet nearly in her face. Then the explosion occurred, causing her to back up with a fright. Turning, the trophy striper sizzled out into deep water, towing Barbara's line, erasing all doubt in her mind as to what was happening.

He was beside Barbara within seconds, whispering encouragement while the poor girl hyperventilated with excitement. Why not? This was a great striped bass, Barbara's first. Zzzzzz—line melted from the reel.

"Easy, Barb," George cautioned, "your line is down a little, so you have to loosen the drag because that makes the reel tighter." These were things that George knew about fighting a good fish, and he coached her every step of the way. Then a light appeared in the eastern horizon, changing in intensity as the vehicle bounced on the sand trail. It was a sight that George had read many times. Knowing that she would never have this monster, this dream fish, in and away before it rounded the curve of the beach, George's greatest fear was unfolding—having someone catch them catching.

The great bass was at least half a spool out into the currents that flowed the deep water outside, dogging and trying to muster enough power to pull free, and Barbara's rod was bent into an arc.

Then the lights of the vehicle were on both of them as George sought to create a little space, make things seem more natural, more like the dead that fishing most often is like.

"Drop your tip, Barbara," he admonished, seeming irritated that she did not know enough to do so herself. She lowered the rod. When the lighthouse completed another revolution, they both looked as though not a thing in fishing was happening. They were two boring silhouettes standing at the sea's edge and the buggy passed without even a notice. Then, as the vehicle faded safely out of sight, Barbara cranked a few turns to find her fish. She cranked a lot of turns—maybe a spool and a half of turns—and her plug clanked harmlessly in the gravel. Her fish was gone. By dropping her tip, she had violated the all-abiding universal law of anglers everywhere: "Do not give slack to a fish." She probably would have caught it otherwise. Here is what Barbara told me:

"I don't get it, Frank. We spend the whole summer casting for these stupid fish. I mean that they have to be stupid when you look at some of the morons out fishing for them who do quite well, really. All you ever hear is that you have to keep a tight line. Finally, after eight million freaking casts, I got this monster that is over four feet long on my line. I know, I saw it! Will you explain something to me? Will you tell me why it is so important that no one sees us with a bleepin' fish? I mean, what the hell, that is what we are out here for.

Catch a fish and keep a tight line, right? I would rather have someone *see* it and catch me catching it than not catch me catching
nuthin'. Like, hello? What is wrong with this picture, here? Why am
I dropping my tip to give slack line? *Worse*, this jeep that is going by
doesn't even have fishing rods. The guy is taking his girlfriend out on
the beach without rods because he has something else in mind. Do
you really think my catching a 50-pounder is going to change that?
Hello?"

Four

Methods for Moby Stripers

WHEN I DID RESEARCH for my last book, *Striper Hot Spots*, I had to rely upon knowledgeable contacts for some parts of the striper coast, such as New Jersey, Long Island, and parts of Maine. After spot selection, one of my guiding considerations was to determine as accurately as possible not what I recommended, but what methods the regulars who fished these hot spots used. I expected to hear the whole gamut of methods, from fly fishing to worm dunking, and largely that is pretty much what turned out. But in the end, do you know what turned out to be overwhelmingly the most popular method? Chunks.

Chunks on the bottom was a method used in virtually every state. Even in places where other methods dominated, chunks were still mentioned as a secondary option. Chunks of what? It depends upon what is around. If it were spring near the estuaries, then chunks of

My wife, Joyce, with a 42-pounder that took a chunk. Chunk baits are the most popular method on the striper coast.

herring or alewife would be used; otherwise it was chunks of mackerel. If bunker (or pogies or menhaden—they're all the same fish) were in the area, then these made a suitable chunking bait. While less popular, I have even seen chunks of bluefish put to use. A piece of the forage fish is cut, laced to a hook on a "fishfinder rig," and sinkered to the bottom. Then you wait. With some anglers—maybe the ones over the edge—there is even a hierarchy of chunk sections: Heads are preferred over tails or center pieces. There are localized variations—in the Cape Cod Canal, for instance, smaller egg sinkers drag the bait down in the current while the chunk is drifted—but the technique is largely on the bot-

MY FAVORITE TROPHY-STRIPER LURES

1. Finnish swimmers—Rebels, Rapalas, Mambos, Red Fins, Bombers
2. Red Gill teasers—all sizes, but 4½ inches is the best
3. Slug-Gos, Fin-S fish
4. Traditional plate swimmers—Atoms, Dannys, GTs, Pikies, jointed eels
5. Jigs with squid strips, rinds, plastic tails
6. Skin plugs
7. Needlefish
8. Tin—Kastmaster, Hopkins, variants
9. Poppers—Swipers, Strikes, Pencils, Reverses

tom. Fresh bait is better, but if that is not available, it is possible to catch bass with fish that were in the freezer, providing that the bait was fresh-frozen and not in the freezer too long. Stripers don't take stinky baits, carrion, or roadkill.

You have to wonder if contemporaries didn't simply rediscover chunking. What they are doing with the method is the same thing their fathers did with "cut bait," an option in widespread use since the advent of sporting tackle. Only the name was changed.

Surfcasting lore is loaded with opinions of the various methods, which largely spring from regional bias. On the Cape's Nauset Beach there is so much sea worm fishing that plugs rarely come out of the package. In Connecticut only children fish with worms. New York surfcasters fail to understand why you would want to baby-sit live eels when rigged ones, which require no care, work so much better. In Rhode Island, if you don't fly fish, you ain't fishin'. In Provincetown on Cape Cod, if you don't plug, you are a weirdo. What is best?

First, everything works. Just about all the traditional methods that catch schoolies will take trophy stripers. Yes, there are a lot of old saws in striper fishing: "Big bait, big fish"; "The big ones are under the schoolies, or [a variation] under the bluefish." Therefore, the monsters are on the bottom. Another: "You have to use live bait." In reality no such general-

Just about all the traditional methods that catch schoolies will take trophy stripers.

izations can be made. Caught by me, gaffed, or weighed for others, I have seen 50-pounders taken on everything mentioned above. Only fly fishing has failed to show me a 50-pounder (I have seen a few in the 40s), but that's because the method was used less when others were catching monsters in the old glory days. Remember, widespread use today reflects the fish that are available now.

No doubt some methods offer a higher success rate because of their efficiency or their natural match with a particular environment. The first thing boat fishers do is install a live-bait well so that they can keep live, free-swimming pogies, mackerel, herring, or pollack. They've learned that the lure of a live bait is too much for even the wariest bass. As a result, many surfcasters have imitated boaters with resourceful live-bait tanks and wire baskets. However, the tail may be wagging the dog here. If surfcasting is favored for its simplicity, then seawater sloshing around in your 35K sport utility may be proof that you need a boat.

The best free-swimming live bait for surfcasters is the eel, because it can be kept alive without a tank, can be purchased easily, and can be carried in the highly mobile setting in

MY FAVORITE TROPHY-STRIPER BAITS

1. Chunks on the bottom (your father's cut bait)—alewives, menhaden, mackerel, mullet
2. Live eels
3. Free-swimming live baits—alewives, menhaden, mackerel
4. Rigged eels
5. Fresh sand eels on the bottom with a sinker
6. Sea worms on the bottom with a sinker
7. Squid, usually frozen

Live eels are popular with striper fishers because they catch stripers.

which surfcasters function. Instead of spending your time foraging for live bait, you pay for it. What you need is a cool, damp container where water cannot build up to later become oxygen deficient. When you walk the beach, eels can be carried in a damp canvas bag that you can dunk periodically. A useful size of eel is around 15 inches; it will weigh just over 3 ounces. This sounds long, but the bait is thin and can be taken readily by even small fish. Use a 7/0 short-shank hook without bait holders; you don't need another little point pricking a fish's mouth when it moves off with the bait.

I have never sinkered an eel to the bottom, although I am aware that some do this. When cast and retrieved, an eel acts as though it were being "plugged" slowly, or at about a third of a swimming plug's speed. The issue of when to hit the fish on the take is fraught with both contention and trade-offs. If the bait is being held, it is in the predator's maw, and you can set the hook as soon as you detect a take; however, hooks can slide right past the lips this way. Your other choice is to allow sufficient time for the taker to swallow it—often, but not necessarily, a count of 10. Deep-hooked this way, a striper would have to break the line in order to be lost. Even if the hook were to pull free of the gullet, there is a chance that it would embed itself in the maw on the way out. Nonetheless, deep-hooked fish are far less likely to survive, and cutting the leader to leave a hook in a fish is equally risky, distinctly unacceptable. Moreover, I have found stripers to be prone to dropping an eel after a few seconds of run; they will drop the bait on a count of 6 when I am planning to set the hook on 10. Some surfcasters will tell you that dropping the eel is the act of small fish, and no doubt it sometimes is. But it's also the action of a dream fish that has felt the hook. Big fish sometimes drop eels.

My New York friends on the Cape used to love to tell the story of the Long Island charter skipper who was fishing live eels and had a client experience a pickup—only to have the bass, a decent one in the 30-pound class, eject the eel through its gills. Whereupon a *sec-*

ond striper picked up the bait, stringing the first on the line. Both decent bass were boated. I don't make this stuff up.

In the old Intrepid Striper Club of Franklin, Massachusetts, one of the gang showed up at a club meeting with a cartoon of two members pulling like the dickens on a striper whose maw was being stretched by two lines in both directions from above by guys on each side of a boat with bent rods. The bass had taken *both* eels.

My first 50-pounder was caught on an eel in Westport, Massachusetts, in 1964. With 20-pound spinning gear and a low-

My first 50-pounder was caught on an eel in Westport, Massachusetts, in 1964. I wanted it but I was afraid to grab it.

TEN COMMON PLUG-FISHING ERRORS

1. Dull or rusty hooks that will break at their bend.
2. Too much terminal junk. Failure to tie direct.
3. Too rapid a retrieve, creating frantic swimming action.
4. Use of wire leaders while *striper* fishing. (A variation of #2, above.)
5. Short dropper leaders on teaser rigs. These inhibit the take of a big fish.
6. Plugs chosen for distance instead of catching qualities.
7. Excessive reliance on poppers, which are glamorous but largely unproductive.
8. Using a teaser or dropper with "fire" (phosphorescent plankton) in the water.
9. Failure to take depth into consideration in lure choice.
10. Failure to inspect for manufacturing flaws: leakers, untempered hooks, swimmability.

capacity reel, I was only able to feed about 150 yards of line into the current of a falling estuary before I ran out. The strategy of the time dictated that I keep at least 50 feet of line on the reel for feeding to a pickup. However, after fishing for a while, it occurred to me that it was better to probe the remaining 50 feet and lose than to guarantee my loss by saving line. Just as I let out the last of the line, a fish picked up the eel. So there I was with 20-pound line and an empty spool with a hard-pulling fish, my hand on the reel, the line in my hand. You don't want to fight a good fish from the point where the line is tied to the bottom of the spool, because that is a weak spot on most rigs. Luckily the line held long enough for me to put some back on by walking out to the top of my waders in the current of the outflow. It was a scary situation.

By that time, age 28, I had done a lot of fishing with my father—sea worms off the Warren River Bridge, baits in dories in upper Narragansett Bay, as well as shiners in sweet water among lily pads. Still, I didn't know much about surf fishing, and I had no way of knowing what the heck I had on. Maybe a shark? Might it get mad at its tormentor and attack once it was in the shallows? Keep in mind that it was midnight and though I have never been afraid of the dark, I still couldn't see. Anyway, after 20 minutes of back and forth, pump and reel, drag slipping, this thing was in the shallows just finning. I wanted it but I was afraid to grab it. Now—with me up on the top of the beach, and it washing up on the shore because it was tired and a light surf wave had pushed it—was the most dangerous time. Afraid to get it until *it* was identified, I put my light on. It was the biggest striper I had ever seen. All I had to do was pick it up. My wife and kids were in the buggy asleep and I woke them with the excitement. Our twin girls, who were four then, were afraid of it and began to cry. It was way bigger than either of them. I knew that striped bass got that big, but always for someone else. My 52-pounder would have cost a dollar an inch back then to mount. I sold it to a restaurant for five dollars. My picture was in the newspaper, and I felt like a big surfcaster after that.

An effective variation in eel fishing is to rig a dead eel; leftovers from a night of live-eel fishing can be used in this way. You will need a rigging needle, which can be made from a 10-inch or so section of coat hanger. Sharpen one end, then forge the opposite end flat and drill a hole to attach line. Run a section of wire leader of the appropriate length from the eel's vent up to its mouth. Then put a 9/0 Siwash hook down the throat and another at the vent. Both hooks should come out the bottom of the bait, straight down to act as a keel. The hooks are then sewn into place at the throat of the hook and at the bend of the hook. Once the bait is finished, bend the eel back

TEASER FACTS

By definition a *teaser* or *dropper* is a nearly weightless lure that is placed in front of a heavier artificial. Any fly or small, light rubber lure will usually work as a teaser if it has a hook suitable for big stripers. Ideally the casting weight would be a lure that casts well and is popular with bass. Still, even when both are good choices for lure fishing, the teaser usually takes more fish than the plug. As the two are retrieved, the teaser is traveling ahead of the plug. Many regulars believe that the plug appears to be stalking the smaller teaser and that the lineside seeks to deprive the plug of the little baitfish. I don't subscribe to that notion, because I have resorted to using a sinker for a casting weight on nights when the sea was all foam from an onshore gale and watched those cows latch onto the teaser. When using this teaser-and-plug system, however, be ready for an occasional double; when the fish are large this can cause one of them to break off. Never fish with more than one teaser; do you want to fight three cows?

People tend to rig teasers to suit their own comfort rather than the needs of taking fish.

What they usually do is tie something that is too short. Instead, you should tie the two lines leading to weight and teaser to the lower ring of a two-way swivel connecting the other ring. Three-way swivels are not necessary. The line to the weight should be at least 5 feet long to allow room enough for a good fish to take the dropper without having its flanks scratched by the hook of the plug or weight. The dropper leader should be at least 18 inches long so as not to interfere with a gulplike take. This sounds cumbersome, but on big fish it works better. Short rigs will cull you into short fish.

This approach will profoundly influence the results of your fishing—but you have to know when *not* to use it. If the sea is full of weeds, you'll lose more time cleaning two things instead of one. If the wind is stopping your casts, teaser outfits will cast even shorter. If there is fire (phosphorescent plankton) in the water, all your junk will turn up so much of it that your plug will look like a canoe, and your little teaser fly will look like a canoe paddle. When the *Pyrodinium* are sparking and glowing at the passage of all that junk, if you put your ear down to the sand, you can hear the bass chuckling and giggling. They are laughing at you.

and forth, cracking its vertebrae, to make it more supple. This will enhance the eel's action on the retrieve.

Among the advantages of using a rigged eel are more weight for casting, a faster sink rate, and the water covering qualities of an artificial. Rigged eels are not fished at all like live ones. They are fished like plugs. Most surfcasters pump an eel at a moderate speed, which is a little faster than that of a swimming plug. However, if you get a lot of motion sense, the feeling that something swiped at it but did not take, increase your speed and you will have more hits. You can keep these baits in your freezer (placed there while your wife is scrubbing the bathtub) for a year or more and refreeze them after trips.

People commonly believe that brute stripers won't take an artificial. That may come from the notion that live bait is *the* thing, so that fake bait is not. Some people prefer to put meat on a hook, toss it into the sea, then wait with two or three additional baited lines. It is a lot easier than throwing an artificial out there and putting enough life into it to fool a big striper by casting and retrieving it until the salt finds its way into the little cuts in your hands. As meat fishing grows more popular, the method is bound to dominate the choices of successful anglers. Artificials, on a per-hour basis, probably do as well as bait, because it is possible to cover more water and be more mobile. In places where the water is moving hard—river mouths or humping tiderips—it is not possible to effectively hold the bottom with a sinker and bait except at slack tide. In many of these waters the fish are moving through, and combing the water with a lure may have advantages over using stationary baits. All situations are different.

When I talk mobility, the notion is not limited to walking a lot. Rather, I mean in every sense. You might go to a creek, for instance, listen, make some casts, then move on to another—even if it's with a vehicle—until you have evidence that stripers are around. Such evidence can be acquired more quickly with a lure. And when it comes to probing, don't overlook the vertical dimension. Shallow water is no problem, because a subsurface swimmer will have it all covered. Yet in some trenches where the water at your fore is deep, choose a lure that you can let down like a bucktail jig. Running depth can be adjusted by jig weight, casting upstream, or sagging a line before you start the retrieve. Heavy jigs (say over 3 ounces, 8/0 in size) with their single hook are a formidably strong choice. No bull bass is going to straighten that sort of thing the way it can the treble hooks on plugs. It has always been a favorite choice of mine to fish some of these fast-water races with a big jig and conventional tackle loaded with 50-pound mono. Another built-in advantage of jigs is that the hook rides up, helping you avoid snags where you are supposed to be fishing—deep. My best jig bass was a 46-pounder from Rhody's Jamestown Bridge. Plugs are something else.

In some areas where bait fishing is popular, there is a belief that huge monsters have to be baited, but this is simply not so. The biggest striper caught following the old Charles Church world record was a 73-pounder taken by Charley Cinto trolling a Goo-Goo Eyes swimming plug. His fish was disqualified for world-record status because it was taken on treble hooks and caught with a wire line. A number of monsters of similar stature have since been taken on plugs. I've had four 50-pound-plus stripers on plugs and untold numbers of big bass that fell short of that. I've been weighing 50-pounders for others as well in areas where plug fishing is *the* thing to do; advancing the notion that trophy stripers will not take a plug there would evoke peals of laughter.

For years we fished the Provincetown second rip just east of Race Point with specially modified swimming plugs that were loaded with lead so that they ran deeper than the subsurface swimmers. We believed that this rip (and there were others, what with 18 feet of water on the end of your cast) yielded better on a deep retrieve. This is not to advocate lead-deadened plugs, because the true quality in a swimming plug lies in its subsurface use; this was a specialized appli-

Charley Cinto with his 73-pounder taken trolling a Goo-Goo Eyes swimming plug. (Photo courtesy Charles E. Cinto)

cation, however. A secondary advantage to the loaded plugs is that they cast better. We cast the heavy plugs, usually Atom 40s or 51s, allowed the slack to be taken up by the sink, then pumped them slowly as they swung downtide and pivoted off the rod tip. Stripers ate the plugs on the swing, not the retrieve.

A killer swimming plug from the old days was the Junior Atom. This was a smaller version of a swimmer (to accommodate spinning tackle)—just under 2 ounces. What Bob Pond, the inventor and manufacturer, was apparently doing with his new version of the Atom plug was imitating an earlier success for the "coffee grinder" bunch. Later he came out with a sort of limited-edition, small-production-run model of the Junior Atom that was loaded at around 2¾ ounces and could be fished comfortably with either spinning or conventional equipment. Of course, like all loaded plugs, the thing had barely, if any, swim to it. It sank like a stone.

I don't know what caused me to reach for this lure in the plug valise of my old buggy in 1966. It was an icy October morning, Green Hill, Rhode Island, predawn. I had a piece of frozen squid on the bottom in a sand-spiked rod, the same low-capacity outfit that I had gotten the 52-pounder with two years earlier, back when I was an amateur. But now that I was a big gun, I had *two* fishing poles. I was plugging with the loaded Junior on my new rig when a fish took the plug close to the beach. Now this thing was taking line and going east toward my squid rod, and I followed until I got to the line. Question: Did she swim under the baited line because she was close to the shore, or did she go over? Going under, I eyeballed the outfit hoping that my choice was right, because I didn't need a nice striper towing my only other surf rod into the suds. Anyway, after a ton of back and forth, this fish was rising and falling in the first wave, and I pressed her toward the shore just as a wave broke. On her side in the foam, she slid back down the bank seaward and I, fearing that I might press her too hard, let her out for a better chance, a subsequent wave. Seconds later, because this thing was about spent, I pressed her a little harder as a curl rose and broke on the banking and my 51-pounder was up, the water down. Running to her, I heard a tinkle in the dark gravel—the plug fell out of her. I was able to grasp her by the gills and haul her up without ever knowing where I had hooked her. This gets better.

Nearly a year later, 2 miles west on East Beach Charlestown, I went out to the back pond to fetch my eels for the night when I found my eel car empty, the door open. Somebody had either felt bad for the eels or had wanted them for his own fishing. All I could do was plug fish—second choice at that time, because this beach was famous for its live-eel fishing. While picking out a plug, I noticed my old friend, the loaded Junior Atom, source of my previous 51-pounder (see above). Even though I knew that this was a catching plug, I had the gnawing back-of-the-mind sense that because it sank like a stone, no action, it was a dog. Depressed by the loss of my favored baits, I just did not give a darn anymore. Snipping the eel hook from the mono, I tied the Junior Atom directly on and went plugging at sunset. No special spot, no special knowledge of where stripers should be plugged, no consciousness of tide. I had been casting and retrieving for 15 minutes or so when I hooked a nice striper . . . another 51-pounder! I had only

EQUIPMENT CHOICES

Most surfcasters fish with heavy spinning tackle that is rated for use on 30- or 20-pound-test mono. Rods should not exceed 9 feet in length because few people, if any, can swing one that's longer. If you want to swing the casting weight through a longer arc, then leave more line trailing from the tip on your cast. Your reel should have a capacity of at least 250 yards and should not deplete dramatically from the loss of line in your average cast. A spool diameter of 2½ inches or more will accomplish this. One-piece rods, while harder to store and carry, have a more uniform full-length action. Select a rod that was designed primarily for casting and not for shipping in a small container. Be sure that the largest possible first, or collector, guide is as close as possible to the spool size of the reel. All guides after that should be ceramic or the like to resist abrading the line. Having a spare spool for your reel is like having another reel, because most problems you'll incur while fishing will be related to your line.

Conventional or revolving-spool reels, when combined with fly gear, make up the other 10 percent of tackle choices. Said differently, "conventional tackle" is not really conventional at all. Here are the pros and cons of revolving-spool reels: They backlash, override, and snarl. The line will wear a groove in your thumb. They break down more often. The line has to be wound onto the spool evenly. Why is conventional-reel fishing the choice of serious surfcasters who want to win? All other things being equal, why not choose a method that will cast farther and enable you to use lines of twice the strength? This book is about dream stripers. You decide.

fished this plug twice, but with it I had taken *two* moby striped bass—among the best 10 or 20 surf stripers on the entire striper coast for their respective seasons. Any knowing surfcaster would have given both of what he held most dear for these fish. I never fished that sinking Junior again. Who can explain it?

Five

Fly Fishing the Striper Surf

THIS IS NOT A BOOK ON FLY FISHING. However, there has been a recent increase of interest in fly fishing overall, and for striped bass in particular. Before the moratorium, the activity was limited to a negligible group of hardcores. Since then growing numbers of stripers—which are most vulnerable to the fly—have become available as suitable quarry for growing number of fly fishers.

A myth I should dispel quickly is that fly fishing is light tackle—that it is schoolie fishing. Few big stripers are taken on flies because very little competent fly fishing, as a percentage of the whole of striper fishing, is being done, even today with the method more widely accepted. Fly fishing in the salt has a short history compared to the other options in widespread use. There is some stunt fishing, often touted in the angling media—raising a fish with casting tackle then presenting a fly—which makes negative statements about the pro-

ductivity of fly fishing. Also, there are some monumental errors being made that are extensions of old sweet-water angling traditions. People often will not fish in strong winds, which is silly, because that can be done by competent fly fishers. There is resistance to fishing at night among fly fishers, because, for many, there is something counterintuitive to the tossing of a small offering into the darkness. Even today fly fishing, now beginning to gain acceptance on striper beaches, remains the last choice for many. One thing that drags the option down is that often the wrong people are doing it without the right reasons. It is not my intention to disapprove of fly fishing the salt chuck. To do so would be to berate not only myself but my wife, our children, and our friends, who all appreciate being able to repeat a cast without interrupting it with a retrieve. Among the many things that

IGFA Men's Fly-Fishing World Records

Tippet Class	Weight	Catch Place	Catch Date	Angler
2 lb	12 lb	Napatree Beach, RI	9/27/97	Alan Caolo
4 lb	19 lb 8 oz	Misquamicut Beach, RI	8/6/97	Alan Caolo
6 lb	24 lb 12 oz	American River, CA	12/2/73	Alfred Perryman
8 lb	42 lb	Sacramento River, CA	5/30/86	Ronald S. Hayashi
12 lb	64 lb 8 oz	Smith River, OR	7/28/73	Beryl E. Bliss
16 lb	51 lb 8 oz	Smith River, OR	5/18/74	Gary L. Dyer
20 lb	33 lb	Chatham, MA	7/23/96	David W. Rimmer

(Courtesy: International Game Fish Association)

IGFA Women's Fly-Fishing World Records

Tippet Class	Weight	Catch Place	Catch Date	Angler
2 lb	VACANT			
4 lb	3 lb 4 oz	Virginia Beach, VA	11/10/98	Vivian M. Webb
6 lb	VACANT			
8 lb	1 lb 14 oz	Virginia Beach, VA	11/1/98	Vivian M. Webb
12 lb	2 lb 8 oz	Virginia Beach, VA	11/8/98	Vivian M. Webb
16 lb	2 lb 4 oz	Virginia Beach, VA	11/8/98	Vivian M. Webb
20 lb	13 lb	Virginia Beach, VA	1/3/98	Stephanie Gooch

(Courtesy: International Game Fish Association)

can be said for the method is that it is an infinitely more pleasurable way to fish and doesn't require any fishing action at all to be enjoyable. Unlike standing passively beside baited rods, the technique is essentially active. Moreover, the take comes to your hand, never your rod, which is more intimate, more participatory. Most of all, there will be times—as with every method in this book—when the fly is the most favorable way to fish, the best choice. No technique is all things to all situations.

In my experiences giving fly-fishing seminars, I've mainly dealt with two groups: competent striper fishers who knew little or nothing about fly fishing and proficient fly fishers who knew little or nothing about stripers. The majority of my students are of the latter calling: They don't know enough about striped bass. In order to effectively take on any species, though, you must understand as much as you can about your adversary. You have to know that predators are more willing to risk the shallows at night. Also crucial is understanding the natural history of your target species—their size potential, arrival and departure seasons, and prey—along with knowing how to read a beach and its structure, as well as the influence of tide. I'm somewhat distressed at the sight of people wearing $2,000 worth of fly-fishing fashions and fishing in the daytime without a clue about where they should be, a full month before the arrival of migratory quarry, curling 90-foot iambic pentameters into an empty sea. I would like to see more informed fly fishing in the striper surf by people who are ready to have something zip into their backing. What we need are dirt-under-the-fingernails commando types who know enough not to put lights on, and enough to listen to the sweet song of the high surf for the occasional note of a striped bass pigging on baitfish in the first wave.

I came to know the fly as it applied to striper fishing in the surf as one of those delightful accidents of fishing. Thirty-five years ago my friends and I discovered that a small tuft of bucktail wound around a single hook often caught as much as the larger plug that we used as a casting weight. The teaser or dropper, as it was known long before I saw it used at the shore, enjoyed a disproportionate level of success. Many midwatch nights, when the linesides poured in over the outer bars by the hundreds, we would all hook up at once. Yet, when we landed our fish, many over 20 pounds, they were impaled upon the teaser, not the plug. We were so impressed with this that we sought to improve the fly with virtually no attention given to its delivery. Because the baits before us were sand eels, which are slim and wispy, we changed from bucktail to saddle hackle for our teaser dressings, later adding color along the flanks and black on top for realism. While we had not invented teaser or dropper fishing, our learning of how effective flies could be was instrumental in the evolution of the larger picture of striper behavior when it came to flies. Still, we had not yet picked up on the importance of presentation.

At this point in the mid-1960s, with roughly 15 years of fly fishing in sweet water under my belt, it was only natural for me to want to give

MY FAVORITE TROPHY-STRIPER FLIES

1. Sand eel flies with four to seven white saddle hackle feathers—easy casting, simulate bait.

2. Clouser Minnow—black is best. These flies run deep, ride hook-point up, and are heavy to cast.

3. Deceivers, all colors—old stand-bys that use bucktail and feathers.

4. Sliders—attention getters that leave a V-wake. They're good in current.

5. Epoxy minnows—short on wispiness, but resilient and realistic looking.

6. Shrimp patterns—highly variable, but good in estuaries with picky fish.

7. Crab patterns—major when you can't figure out what stripers are eating at Monomoy.

8. Cinder worms—simple, reddish fakes that still fail to compete with real worms.

9. Popping and skipping bugs—watch for followers that won't take with these.

10. Big bunker patterns—these fool stripers, but are hard to cast because of their size and wet weight.

stripers a go with fly tackle. I had heard of people doing this, and I had read a few articles in magazines. What we never anticipated was that the fly would be even more effective when fished without the distraction of the plug following it. But we learned quickly that a lone fly, when delivered through true fly-fishing methods, could in fact outfish flies delivered ahead of plugs by five to one, maybe more.

As commercial anglers, in those days the profit motive was our greatest incentive. We didn't use seines because they were against the law; we didn't use dynamite because we didn't know how or where to get it. When bass were difficult, picky, and demanding, we fly fished. It wasn't for fly fishing's sake; we chose it because it was almost as good as nets and dynamite.

A lot has changed since then. Not in the natural requirements of coastal fly fishing—angling conditions and our target species' traits—but in the equipment we use to deal with them.

The curse of big-game fly fishing is weight. Unlike other methods, we still fly fish the surf with a one-handed rod. We thus cast with

Two basic disciplines come together here: fly fishing and striper fishing.

one arm for fish that are sought with two-handed equipment by everyone else. When we false-cast a 10-weight line, that lone arm can go bad quickly because of the combined weight of the fly tackle. Here is the problem.

In order to be protected from the run of even a moderate striper, you will need at least 200 yards of braided backing. Mono cannot be used as backing, because it will contract and crush the spool. This amount of braid, when added to the bulk of the fly line, requires a large-capacity spool; indeed, the fly reel is the heaviest item in the outfit. You may swing the rod, but it is the reel that is the true weight. The challenge becomes one of finding ways to increase backing without enlarging the reel—and there really aren't any.

The largest possible leader is 20-pound test, which is often needed to take on fish in the 40-pound-and-up class. Everything else in the equipment must be substantially stronger than that tippet. Otherwise, weak spots developing in the backing—braid decay, knot strength, or fishing damage—could fall below the tippet strength. It is imperative that the tippet remain the weakest point in your chain of equipment, from hook to spool bottom. On paper 30-pound backing sounds suitable, but knot strength of anything less than that, along with backing's tendency to decay after a few weeks of dampness, render this too close to leader strength. Considering that we change leaders often in order to keep them in top condition, it is easy to envision the backing strength falling below that of the leader. And it is one thing to break your leader, losing the fish, fly, or a couple of feet of tippet. It is quite another to break off in your backing and bid adieu to the entire fly line and perhaps even the night's fishing. Unlike mono, braided line is offered in limited size increments. Still, some of the new small-diameter materials that test at 40 or 50 pounds might permit a long-enough backing without too large a reel to weigh you down. Naturally a reel small enough to fish with comfortably, with suitable backing, should be equipped with a big-game drag.

When there are many schoolies around, or in inland estuaries where moby linesides are less likely, you will often be tempted to reduce your tippet size. However, if you bend on a section of 10- or 12-pound leader at the fly and Mr. Big comes along, don't say I did not warn you. The ocean holds many surprises that play no small part in the charm of saltwater fishing. No doubt suitable knotless tapered leaders are close to development by the big tackle companies, but I haven't seen any at this writing. As a result I fashion my own by joining sections of 40 pound, then 30, and 20—3 feet, 2 feet, and 3 feet respectively (The last section goes long again to provide material for changing flies.) Trout and salmon fishermen accustomed to leaders of up to 15 feet may be uncomfortable with these shorter leaders. Nevertheless, they will thank me when handling heavier flies. Remember that the bass are selective but not leader-shy.

In other applications the rod enjoys two functions: casting and fighting. In big-game fly fishing, however, the fighting function of the rod—its normal mission of absorbing the forces of pulling on a fish— falls far short. With all but the smallest fish, the rod is bent over so hard most of the time that it can neither give any more nor respond to reductions in force. I have often taken pictures of fly fishermen fighting stripers with rods over so hard that they appeared to have something tethered to a rope. It is therefore unnecessary to endure the added weight of higher-rated rods and their resultant heavier lines. This begins to have meaning for people like my wife and our grown daughters, who don't lift weights. They do fine, for a few hours anyway, with 9-foot rods rated for 8-weight lines. Adult males probably can fish a strong wind with a $9\frac{1}{2}$-foot 10-weight. Make sure that your rod has a fighting butt, which is necessary to take the weight off your shoulders and move a wildly rotating reel away from your body and clothes. Most fly rods come with snake guides on the tip section, but if you are using a mono running line with a shooting head, consider replacing them with ceramic guides.

Saltwater fishing, particularly from shore, wreaks havoc with fly rods. You'll drop them, bounce them on the jetty stones, forget them on the roof of your SUV, and have coils of stripping foul after a take, ripping the guides off. Consequently, I advise against paying too much for top-of-the-line sticks unless you're bent upon punishing your kids for their teenage years by spending their inheritance.

Most of your fly-line needs will be served with a weight-forward floating line. Still, anyone who feels that he should never allow the tragic consequences of failing to own all he might ever need should also have an extra-fast-sinking weight-forward. There are bound to be situations—deep tiderips, inlet outflows, presentations to bottom-rooting fish—where getting the fly down quickly is a must. I see no reason to stand around waiting for a line and fly to sink. It is inefficient and results in ineffectual presentations in many situations where current will cause it to drift too high. True, a lineside will come up for and even chase a fly, but you are more likely to get its attention if you can pass the fly more closely to the snout. I elaborate upon sinking lines here, despite their being needed only a minority of the time, because I have always felt that there is less appreciation for their importance than they deserve. People want to fish floating lines because they are easier to handle, easier to pick up. Are you in the striper surf to cast or to fish? Moreover, if anything happens to that floater, you'll wish you had a sinker along to which you could resort.

Because you're fishing from shore, only rarely is reachable water going to be deep enough to require a sinking line to get down to stripers. Still, good angling policy dictates that we be prepared for any eventuality, including swinging through deep runs and fishing deeply on fast-sloping beaches.

Shooting tapers or heads are controversial—many anglers dislike both the difference in their timing on the backcast and their balkiness in a headwind—but they do produce better distances when carrying fine running lines through the guides. I have watched salmon fishers use them for impressive distance casting on wide-open rivers where wind was as much a problem as in the open sea. The knot connecting the head to the running line can be distracting and can feel like a take when it bumps the guides. Most so-called smooth connections compromise strength. Some systems attach heads with a loop-to-loop setup that allows a quick change of heads for different sink rates; I, on the other hand, prefer the option of having fewer of them but on a suitable spare spool or reel. The equipment thing can get out of hand.

In the old-time fly fishing of my youth, the question often came up as to whether the fishing depended upon pattern or presentation. In other words, was it the fly or how you showed it to the bass? We have all seen trout so selective that we have to have exactly the right fly; on the other hand, some have seen Atlantic salmon—notorious nonfeeders—disregard fly pattern and size while taking rabidly any offering that came by at the right speed. Similarly, fishing for striped bass confronts us with any number of pattern and presentation combinations. While both do count, I think that presentation is more important than pattern.

I have always thought that it was more important to be at the right place, the right depth, and the right retrieve speed than fishing with the right fly. They'll take almost anything that simulates a minnow; any streamer that's close in size and shape to what is around. Stripers are often not smart enough to reject a poor imitation. Still, this is not to say that you should be careless in the production of flies, any more than you should be making poor presentations. For instance, in the tying of a diminutive sand eel, pure bucktail tends to be too short, too bushy forward. Saddle feathers, on the other hand, are long enough and slim enough to produce a favorable sand eel impersonation. All-white feathers produce a suitable pattern, but a slice of realism can be introduced with no effort. A darker back and a gradation of color along the flanks can be accomplished by changing feathers for color in the mix. Such simple streamers will solve 90 percent of your pattern needs. But I'd like to elaborate upon the needs of the other 10 percent.

Stripers feed upon many different sizes of bait. I have witnessed explosions of 40-pounders thrashing on 4-pound shad. I have also seen the same monster linesides sipping 1-inch grass shrimp. The variety of bait sizes with which you could be confronted runs well beyond your ability to simulate in a castable fly. As shore fishers we cannot trail line out behind us; we are required to *cast* everything. With casting requirements in mind, enhanced by the notion that zero casting weight is ideal, there are clear weight limits defined by hook size, dressings, and water absorption. You may be able to create an exciting 8-inch alewife pattern at the tying bench—as I have seen so many do—but you are not going to fly fish with it.

The best all-around hook size is probably 3/0. This is small enough to be taken by schoolies yet will handle your biggest lineside. When you are sure that all the fish are small or when you are far enough inland—wherever that is—to be safe from the attack of a

Heavy flies like these will catch stripers, but they are balky to cast.

moby striper, you can enjoy the comfort of a lighter fly in a 1/0 hook size. From here any departure in hook size in either direction begins to get unwieldy. You should not handle 40-pounders with a hook any smaller than a 1/0, but you'll feel dramatic differences in your casting with a 4/0. The weight of the larger hook is double that of the smaller one. Worse, there is a negligible weight difference between the dry materials of the two flies, but once water absorption joins the equation simple flies double in weight. For instance, in an (ahem) scientific study, I soaked a 3/0 mink skin eelet, already on the heavy side, in a glass of water overnight. It doubled to 40 grains. A spun deer hair mullet tripled to 51 grains. Flies for big game have taken on a life of their own these days; we see such out-of-control realism as 6/0 bunker flies. While it pains me to rail at these creations, because no one appreciates the fly tier's art more than I, I am compelled to ask if anyone is planning to throw these things . . . other than with light spinning gear.

Adding epoxy to minnows also adds weight and takes the wispy, weightless quality out of a pattern, but such flies work in the right situation and stand up well to bluefish teeth. Another weighty pattern that acts almost like a jig because of its eyes is the Clouser; it can bomb, but black can be awfully good. If you want the realism of eyes, paint them on. It is counterintuitive to say this, but many times popping bugs get the attention of following stripers, yet fail to be taken. The more subtle sliders, which leave a V-wake, or even a streamer tied to riffle will get attention more quickly with their movement.

During blitzy situations, where bait and gamefish are frenzied close to shore, just about anything that you throw is likely to be taken. What is more exciting than viewing a bass swimming through the side of a wave to take a fly?

Part of today's fly-fishing ethic is the tendency to use barbless hooks. Indeed, it is in the interest of striper fishing's continuation to shake a lineside free undamaged as quickly as possible. Certainly when you're surrounded with undersize fish, which is common, I advise barbless hooks. They allow you to remove shorts more easily, more safely—but keep in mind that their rate of dropping fish is slightly higher. No angler should ever use barbless hooks if there is a reasonable chance of hooking a fish wanted for posterity. Why not fish for the monster of your dreams as though you really wanted to catch it? Such a hook would have a barb.

Regardless of their tackle choice, all striper fishers face the same sets of structure, water, and natural conditions. Some students of fly fishing think their situation is unique because their tackle was purchased in a different place. I think it counterproductive to cop out on a night, location, set of conditions, or season because you're fishing with a fly. Those who cry about a strong onshore wind need a long spinning rod and a new therapist. Let's look at striper water as it applies to all fishing, including the fly.

Moving water solves all of a striper's feeding problems, because it conveys bait. Along open beaches, though, such tiderips are difficult to isolate from the geographical mix. Thus, beach fishing—fly or otherwise—requires a more refined understanding of how to determine changes in the structure, be they bars, holes, sloughs, or the narrows left by the placement of islands. Worse, on some shores everything looks the same. Concerns about distance casting on wide-expanse shores need not worry the fly fisher, because the best opportunity will be in the first wave or just beyond. Places that exhibit more structure will force water to move this way or that, and a well-placed fly will take advantage. For instance, water may be breaking over an outer bar then sliding into a hole before building a seaward current out of its opening. A few casts behind the bar, a few into the hole, a few into the seaward sliding slough and you have a feel for the water's life and hopefully for where the bass are holding. There is notable fishing on some rocky shores (such as Montauk, Narragansett, and Newport, Rhode Island) or even on any of a thousand jetties. Such nook-and-cranny shorelines offer suitable cover for baitfish and great hunt-and-trap foraging opportunities. Most rock structures change very slowly, so competent observation will pay off for a long time. Remember that there are often hazards associated with fishing from rocks, where a bad step can kill you. Also, getting a trophy striper up from a high rocky perch can be a problem. It is a good idea, then, to find suitable landing options *before* you start fishing. Sand and stones out of the way, striper water gets easier.

In the continued search for moving water, inlets are known to be reliable producers of good bass fishing. (I cover these in chapter 8.) I would advise against trying to fly fish the more heavily fished spots, as fly fishing, a minority choice, may conflict with traditional methods. But smaller inlets, often less popular, can be fished effectively. Work the insides of such inlets, during any tide, much the way you would fish a river.

Because they are anadromous—which means freshwater spawners—stripers are highly estuarine. They think little of running shallows with barely enough water to cover their backs. Consequently, if there is enough of such protection as depth or darkness, they will splash about in the bays, rivers, coves, and tidal marshes of our coast in search of easy bait and the moving water that conveys it. Such estuaries protect anglers from sea storms, provide flat water and access to more docile environments, and fly fish as nicely as a Maine beaver pond. There is usually current, and the depth varies with tide. Much estuarine fishing is "flats" fishing—a term borrowed from the South, where it is done more for other species. In many inland tidewater locations, it is possible to wade flats in the night and hear the slurps, or see the dark gray stains, of feeding linesides feasting in wadable shallows. Here the fly fisher spot-casts to a target, watches his quarry turn, hears it slurp, then feels the tug and pull. Fly fishing and stripers give each other a good name.

Top to bottom: Sand eel, Deceiver, two Clousers, slider, piping sand eel, shrimp, popping bug, cinder worms.

That is not to say that all fly fishing on striper flats is romantic and easy. One of the greatest frustrations is to be surrounded by line-sides on the flats when they are feeding on cinder worms. When such a hatch of sea worms (*Nereis* spp.) takes place, the preponderance of bait can bring hundreds if not thousands of gamefish, which slurp and gulp audibly. I call this frustration because when it occurs, the water is dotted every foot with a worm, and such a lode of bait is way more than a bass can eat. You and your fly are in competition with a million juicy worms, and the stripers are turning and slurping at a rate that suggests there are more around than are truly there. Worse, when you hear a slurp 25 feet out, you cast there—and the bass is long gone, sipping another worm. Your mind says that you should be catching a bass every cast, but reality spawns frustration once it sinks in that you are surrounded by gamefish and catching nothing. Such worm hatches take place more often in spring, but I have suffered them as late as August in Rhode Island estuaries. I would much prefer to fish a quiet spot without bait using a slim streamer that proves to be a target of opportunity for *one* hungry striper. It may be dangerous to think that because the water is smaller in some estuaries, the bass that go there are on the small side. It is a trap that arises from the natural laws of longevity: No matter where we fish, there are usually more small bass. Still, you should be just as ready for a monster lineside here as anywhere else.

If you ever see a big striper tailing in the shallows for sand eels, you'll never forget it. At first sight you'll think of a shark's dorsal fin; however, upon closer examination, what is visible is the top of the lineside's tail tipped at an angle determined by a combination of depth and length of fish. What the feeding bass is attempting to do is retain equilibrium while standing on her nose in water too shallow to support her length. Thus, she will drift first one way to the side, overreact, then swing to the other, much in the way you or I might do were we also to try to stand on our heads. This is not to say that sand-eel-feeding fish always tail. Tailing is but one technique that they use, perhaps in response to sand eel behavior. You'll need a sinking line despite the shallow water; otherwise your fly will pass too high to be mistaken for one of the sand eels being inhaled on the bottom. It is best to make it easy for that old sow of a fish to find your fly. I have seen 40-pounders do this in the shallows of Cape Cod's Race Point Bar in the light of day. Such memorable events in the striper surf will haunt your dreams through the deepest and darkest of winters.

What marine charm lures fly casters from their sweet-water rivers and trout lakes? It is not natural beauty, nor the shortage of trout or challenge. I believe that contemporary fly fishermen are looking for a good fight. They want to smoke a fly reel, see a section of backing that has never been exposed. They want the rush of going so far into their backing that they might run out—something that they've never experienced trout fishing and has happened but rarely while fishing for salmon. Only one fish that requires two hands to carry can be caught regularly with a fly in the northwestern Atlantic. Aren't we lucky that such a delightful accident lives here and that it is the striped bass?

Six

Conditions

MUCH OF WHAT BEWILDERS budding surfcasters relates to fishing conditions and their interrelationships with one another. For instance, it is not enough to understand the influence of tide upon the fishing opportunities in a given spot; you must also understand what tide does when the wind is a certain way. And that is the simple example. What if we take wind, tide, light, season, bait, and a few as-yet undiscovered components and stir them into the conditions mix of a hot spot? How do these influence one another? The possibilities are infinite and the craft is called surfcasting for striped bass.

Intimacy with conditions is what separates those who believe luck is the prime component in angling success and those who unaccountably demonstrate a knack for being in the right place at the right time. In our shopping list of conditions, let's cover tide first.

People are always asking me about my favorite tide. Most seem to believe the "secret" that unlocks successful bass fishing lies in knowing what tide is best. If it were that simple, there wouldn't be a fish left in the ocean. However, there *is* a best tide for many locations, while other spots yield during no particular tide. If a location is of particular interest to you, then make a study of the fishing there at all tide phases and carefully log all known conditions. Look for correlations of environmental factors. For instance, if you are always getting skunked when fishing the drop, note this, along with any observable conditions. Keep in mind that while you may be studying tide, there could come a time when you might want to move to evaluating another condition, and then much of your legwork will be done. Sometimes it is possible to accidentally stumble on a productive condition or set of them. One time an acquaintance told me that, while a certain jetty was productive on the drop, it was even better on the drop coupled with a southeast wind. At the time I didn't take him seriously; later I learned that he was right. Back to tide.

I'm fond of tidal changes: not just the change from rise to fall, but also the change to slack, the beginning of the fall, the times when the water is accelerating in either direction. In some places, especially where the currents are strongest, there is a musical-chairs effect at slack tide when the predators we seek are moving to take up new positions. This additional movement of the stripers is a chance for us to contact those that, hours ago, might have been out of reach.

One of the compensations of being tidewise is that it is possible to cash in on predictable action at Funny Beach and then reposition yourself at Moonlight Bay when the tide is right there. In areas that contain a variety of diverse structures, a number of different spots could present the alert surfcaster a nightlong itinerary of opportunity. The only frustration in knowing what you are doing is that you might have to choose among several locations that are at their best during the same stage of tide.

If people understood the pure cycle in tide, tackle shops would have to hand out lollipops instead of tide charts, because there would be no need for a sheet of paper listing all the days of the year and what the tide is going to do. The tide is fixed by moon phase, so that all you need to know to determine what the tide is doing is know the moon phase. We've moved away from calendars that show moon phases, as we have from many natural things; most calendars don't even show phases anymore. It's the first thing I look for. Here's why.

On the night when the moon is full, the tide at every place on the planet will always be the same as it was the last time the moon was full. It will be different from place to place—say high in Providence at 8:45 P.M. and in Boston at midnight—but the next time you see the white circle on the calendar, that means high water for those cities. If your secret spot is best at low tide, just add or subtract six hours to determine low. Suppose you hit the fish at 10 P.M. Friday night. If you plan to go right back there the next weekend, next Friday night, the tide will be exactly the opposite This is because the tide moves up 50 minutes per day, on average. Thus, if you like fishing at 10 P.M., you'll have to wait two weeks for conditions to match up; and even then the light will be different. Identical light and tide conditions are a month away—a "moonth" away.

The full black circle, the new moon, is when the moon is full at midday. You can go out in the bright sun and see it. At night that gibbous moon will be on the other side of our earth and it will be very dark here as a result. So while you have the same tide as you had two weeks ago, you don't have the same light, the same bright moon. What about the weeks between full and new?

Each night after the full, the tide is high 50 minutes later and the moon rises, edges onto the horizon, that many minutes later. Barely noticeable the first few nights, a little piece of the moon is missing; more goes away each night, until about half is gone. Also, while there is no such thing as a "half" moon, that phase is called the last quarter and occurs seven nights after full. A half portion rises in the deep night to change light. This light is not as bright as a full moon. It's more subtle; moreover, it represents a change in conditions that most of your friends will miss. Remember that the tide is exactly opposite that which you experienced during full and new. More importantly, you will have another night in two weeks with the same tide, but the half moon will be shadowed on a different side and, instead of rising at that hour, it will set. Again, a change in conditions, a change in light to a more darkened situation.

I've never been able to determine if it was the stage of tide or the change of light that accounted for it, but both quarter-moon situations have produced good fishing for me with an uncanny regularity. In the deep night, say 2 A.M., that sliver of last quarter moon on the horizon triggers a rise in the fishing that continues until dawn. Two weeks later, during the first quarter, fishing always ends when the moon sets. Fishing with a number of Cape Cod regulars on many of the same beaches nightly, I saw a lot of the gang make the mistake of quitting before a productive condition presented itself. Most of them, tired from having fished the full moon and a few nights of its decline, often went to bed forgetful of the rising or setting moon.

Light is a powerful factor in locating cooperative stripers, because they require protective cover to venture into the hazards of the surf. For that reason serious surfcasters should do most of their fishing at night. Yes, you can catch stripers in daylight, but chances diminish. Moreover—and remember that this book is about *big* stripers—truly large linesides, while rare in the day, are common at night. Protective cover for bass can be found in a number of forms—deep water, heavy surf, and reduced light all contribute to a safe environment in which bass will forage. I've seen all the combinations produce. The deep water is one reason why people in boats do better. You will see daytime blitzes, but they are more likely in a rough sea. Calm nights will work in the shallows without moonlight. If they're in a favorable feeding situation, overly excited fish that started working during the night will often linger, seemingly more willing to take risks; but there usually has to be an incentive for them.

An interesting social consideration is that many fishing writers, forced to illustrate their own work as I have been, fear night photog-

You will see daytime blitzes, but they're more likely in a rough sea. I've seen all the combinations of fishing conditions produce.

raphy. Believing that there is no color in darkness, they lack the exposures to properly illustrate surf fishing the way it should be depicted. Thus, nighttime, the most important time, is often not given the vigorous attention that it deserves in illustration. Through implication,

DOES BAIT MEAN BASS?

As fishers we are taught to look for bait, because it is believed that stripers will be with the bait. Which is true, but not always so. One night we came upon a windrow of dead squid that stretched in both directions as far as we could walk. The baitfish, roughly a foot long, lay dead on the water's edge, with some of the fresher ones still kicking. However, even those we returned beached themselves immediately. So we impaled some on our hooks and cast them into what we believed would be a sea filled with stripers. Nothing. We drove our beach vehicle a mile east past hundreds of pounds of more squid and bottom-fished again. Still nothing. That night we found 10 miles and many tons of dead squid and nary a lineside. Could the bass have had their fill? At dawn gulls cleaned up the beach so well that they couldn't fly.

this suggests that surfcasting is done more often during the day.

Artificial light can be detrimental to successful surf fishing. We seek wild animals here that are over 20 years old, predators that have learned that they too can be some other creature's food. A consequence is that a sudden burst of light—a flashlight for baiting up or to point the way while wading, or even a smoker's lighter or match—will send a moby fish scurrying for cover. Back when I was a rod-and-reel commercial angler, I often hit fish on some hole on the beach and would notice the lights of a vehicle bouncing the waterline trail in my direction. My wife, Joyce, would sag in the cab feigning sleep and I would fish half-heartedly. Invariably the driver would keep his headlights on in order to observe if there were any fish hidden under the buggy. Once he was past—and I've experienced this many times—there would be no stripers in that hot hole for 10 to 15 minutes. They were all blown temporarily to deeper water by the passing vehicle. I have also been caught with an uptight rod, inadvertently drawing both attention and company. When someone stopped, he'd usually fish a while, then move on, because he had not fished long enough to allow the stripers he frightened out to return.

Artificial light is not necessarily bad if it remains constant or establishes a certain predictable pattern to which bass can become acclimated. The Cape Cod Canal lights, glowing amber for 7 miles on both banks, present no detriment to the fishing. Well-lit bridges and docks create shadows, by-products of light, that appeal to most gamefish and much of their forage. Even lighthouses, which bathe the sea in front of them with light, actually enhance the fishing. Years ago our children used to time their expected hits with the passing of the light's rotation while fishing Race Point. As a family joke, it was known as the "13-second rule." But all bets are off if you are going to move between the light source and water casting a *moving* shadow. Shadow movement is a major part of the controversy that surrounds the use of lanterns while bait fishing.

Phosphorescent plankton can show up on all coasts on any night during the warmer part of the season. Highly variable in intensity, these microscopic organisms have a way of highlighting all that fraudulent junk you've been offering stripers. True, you got away with it nights when no marine life burst white or green with the motion of your offering, or when there was enough natural light to offset the fire, as it is called by surfcasters. Nevertheless, when your plug upsets thousands of these tiny animals as it travels, you're going to catch less. Worse, you learn that something is wrong with your fishing when you see moby bass turn away from your plug in the shallows, a clear sign that instead of taking they have been spooked. When bioluminescence is taken to its extreme, the plug and trailing bass look like a baseball bat being followed by a canoe. This is scary for beginners, particularly when wading flats hundreds of yards from shore. A subtle effect can be induced by slowing your retrieve, fishing smaller, and avoiding teasers, swivels, and wire leaders (all of which upset more fire and highlight your equipment). Even when you deal with fire properly, fishing is rarely as good. People who know that the light is going to change and have made a study of conditions can either avoid the situation or effectively wait it out, because the fire will go out or be reduced once the moon rises.

Despite my urging you to fish at night, it is also imperative that you be prepared to spend some time around water during the day. You could be starting out in the evening or heading home after the dawn. The use of polarized sunglasses, not simply the regular kind, is universal, basic. A simple test to determine the polarizing quality is to place two pairs of sunglasses at 90 degrees to each other; if both are equipped with polarized lenses, all light will be blocked out and blackness will be all you see when you look through them. Polarized glasses allow your eyesight to penetrate surface glare so that you can see bottom structure while reading the beach during the day for later use at night. Moreover, it is possible to see stripers, particularly the kind that this book is about, cruising in the surf at times.

I would never go to the beach in the day to "look" for stripers. Seeing fish from shore is so rare that your resources are far better spent resting during the day for a more productive effort in the night. Still, having emphasized that, let me tell you about some particularly fascinating experiences that teach something of our craft while daylight fishing.

The most common striper sightings occur in autumn during the migration. This is when bass have staged themselves in larger schools, often of similar size. Dropping temperatures and a lowered photo period get them moving south, and the sea is a garden of foraging opportunity. Consequently, you'll often *see* stripers bursting the sea white with explosions as they slam baitfish. One October, during the Rhode Island hickory shad run, I watched bass of over 40 pounds, maybe some to 60, in the first wave. They were eating 2- and 3-pound shad that were lunging onto the wet sand to escape their tormentors. When it is like that, you have to ask yourself how many of the things the bass can eat. Maybe, because we have no measure, they actually catch very few and eat much less as a result. I know that it would surprise the average observer just how large a bait they will take; I have known boat fishers who routinely live-lined 4-pound pollack and mackerel.

A common way to find stripers is to find working birds. These are always a bellwether of action for they have the advantage of looking straight down upon pods of bait while seeing the predators—usually but not necessarily stripers. (Wouldn't you love to know if birds can penetrate surface glare, sort of biological polaroids?) What happens is that the small forage is pushed upward by feeding gamefish, then struck from above by diving birds. It could be that birds drive the bait downward into the feeding fish, which bounce it back to birds in some sort of interspecies cooperative effort. Remember, I've been fishing too long and could be over the edge fishwise.

There is promise on any beach that has bait; thus, its presence deserves watching and should be kept in mind as a strong indicator of potential opportunity. Species depending (and there are hundreds of bait species), bait in daylight often looks dark and can easily be mistaken for weeds or a black spot on the bottom. Don't be put off by unmolested bait; gamefish will either find it or return for it later. Were I to investigate five beaches and find bait on one, I would fish that one the following night.

There is promise on any beach that has bait.

It is possible to walk or drive a waterline and actually see a big bass lolling in the surf. That happened to me one sunset on a loner. I made one cast and the thing just dropped behind my swimmer, accelerated a few pumps, and then ate it. Incidentally, if you ever actually witness a take like that, don't go by what you see but by what you feel, hauling back when you feel it. It is a page from the salmon-fishing manual.

I have often come upon bass along the beach in late fall; fish of all sizes were swimming through the sides of waves in pursuit of bait. The rougher the water, the closer and wilder the linesides performed. In the early 1990s an acquaintance cast tin into the teeth of an onshore gale in Rhode Island for a fish in the low 50s, during a time when few such fish were available. One September dawn I landed a 44-pounder on a rigged eel during a daylight blitz. That morning I saw other big stripers better than the one I had. Those are the good times. Often when fish are stacked like that, it is a case of trying to get through the little fish and hook up to a trophy before one of the lesser ones latches on. It may at times be possible to choose a bait or lure that culls—one too large for small fish but perfect for the monsters. Even then, events often fail to follow the script, and fish only inches longer than the biggest plug in your bag can take it down. You'll hear old sayings like "fish deep," because the big ones are underneath; that is an often-handed-down cliché more than a statement of fact.

I have often seen big bass in the surf just after sunrise when they had extended their activity beyond the night. Sometimes I have found them doing this in early-morning light; other times I had picked them up during the night at some hot spot where I knew enough to look and just stayed with them while the light changed. Maybe they are like us in that when they are having a good time, they hate to quit. Yet they are unlikely to *start* in a risky situation of flat

I have often seen big bass in the surf just after sunrise when they had extended their activity beyond the night.

water, light, and shallows. Worthy of mention is that all species of wildlife increase their activity during the first fire of a new day.

You will locate more bass in the deep night than at any other time, and the detection will be either by sight or sound. Often the soft sibilance of the surf drowns out the slurps and gulps of feeding bass, even the big ones. However, in protected estuaries that are millpond flat, and millpond quiet as a result, you will often hear the feeding action, especially if it is for free-swimmers that can run and be chased. Just how noisy it all is in a quiet setting depends upon the forage and the size of predatory stripers. Large bass, if sipping worms, will sound like small ones; small stripers, if chasing baitfish, will be noisier. So it is not always possible to determine the sizes by sounds alone. Different baits evoke different responses. Whiting runs in the Cape Cod Canal, during periods when moby stripers inhabit Cape

Cod Bay, cause these fish to go so bonkers that a pursuing monster will often sound as though a mule had been dropped from one of the bridges. During an onshore sou'wester that frosted the sea to foam, I once watched decent bass chasing summer squid 15 to 18 inches long. Each time a squid was taken, there was a burst of white that would scare you. When you experience night action with a noisy background, breaks appear as a stain of black on gray.

Big water plays out according to intensity. I'll take a rough sea for surfcasting anytime, because it affords cover and makes baitfish more vulnerable. Moreover, a windswept sea that is onshore tends to

Big water plays out according to intensity. I'll take a rough sea for surfcasting anytime, because it affords cover and makes baitfish more vulnerable.

upwell, causing vertical movement in the water column where the warm surface water is against the beach. Higher water temperatures appeal to and thus often contain lower orders of the food chain. Yet rough water is not always a function of wind.

Passing storms, depending upon intensity and proximity, tend to create swells that can have waves cresting a half mile offshore. And as with too much wind, a wild, out-of-control sea is neither fishable nor safe. Most of the surfcasting deaths of which I have heard occurred under such wild water. The sad thing is that no fish would be caught in those conditions anyway, because a turned-up sea is filled with suspended silt and weed, usually discolored, and so white with foam that an artificial cannot be seen and a bait cannot be held on the bottom. One of the values of a well-rounded angling education is that you know when *not* to fish. A mistake from which, unaccountably, I never seem to learn is fishing during the passing of an offshore hurricane. You are shown a location for one on the weather map. It is way south of Bermuda, thousands of miles away, so you think—because you've been assured that it is not going to strike—it is not a threat. It isn't, but its influence can be felt 2,000 miles across open water in the form of the "Good Vibrations" that the Beach Boys sang about. You could be fishing under a starry sky and be shoved scarily all over the surf line in an inside-out discolored sea that no striper could possibly be found in. The voice of experience here.

Anytime you find yourself blown out by wild conditions from a storm or even a passing hurricane, it is possible to save a trip by fishing inside an estuary, river, or bay. Winds don't have enough space to kick up the water here, and sea swells cannot make it into these protected spots.

Temperatures are not as much of a problem for stripers as they are for us. The first spring linesides, fish so small that they have no place in this discourse, won't be caught until the seawater temperature is over 50 degrees F. By then inland air temperatures, even at night, will rarely drop below freezing. When they do, the sea's mass will prevent air temperatures from getting that low. Many reporters seek to explain temporary bass shortages in summer by blaming "slugs of warm water that cause the stripers to move out." Fairy lore. I've caught bass at between 50 and 72 degrees F, with some of the finest summer fishing that I've ever had at 72. However, fall temperatures can present a set of circumstances while stripers are around in which cold can be a problem. There is considerable lag between water and air temperatures when the season has changed to winter; the temperatures of the previous month are reflected in the sea. West of Cape Cod, from Vineyard Sound to Montauk, it is possible to enjoy water in the high 50s from late November to early December while the land abutting this tepid sea is locked in swirling snow. One year, my first after retirement from a day job, I hunted deer in upstate New York on new snow, then came home and surfcasted for memorable stripers in Rhode Island. The comfort limit for fishing the beach is about 20 degrees F, a temperature that you are not likely to encounter until early December. By then the stripers are usually gone from the northern locations where they are fished. That temperature, approximately 20 degrees, is one that I realized is limiting while fly fishing trout in inland lakes and steelheading, but sea fishing from icy jetties is something about which everyone should think twice. When ice in the guides prevents your retrieve, you might want to turn yourself in to the Frank Daignault Rehab Center for over-the-edge surfcasters where they serve Scotch instead of orange juice at breakfast.

Seven

Games Big Stripers Play

I WON'T TRY to name the age at which stripers begin to play games, but the fish I'm speaking of here are all females so it is probably early. My old Cape surfcasting pal, George Carlezon, used to say that the reason why big stripers are so hard to catch is that they are all females and cannot make up their minds when your plug or eel is passing whether they should take it or not. Just kidding.

In Narragansett, 35 years ago, I hooked a fish on a live mackerel and it gave me the shakes. My tinker was swimming under a plastic lemon float when the bobber disappeared. After waiting a few seconds for the brute to take it down, I set on a fish that tore the line from my squidder. Doing the back-and-forth thing, I started to stow line; I could see from the fish pumping up the side of a wave in daylight that she was close to 4 feet long. Decent. About when she was in my fore, when she could come careening in at any time, she dove straight down. No problem. I had her, she didn't have me. All of a sudden I couldn't move her. For a little while I could still feel something on the end of my line, but then things just got tighter and tighter and I came to realize that I was hopelessly tangled in the bottom. I had to break my line and never saw this cow again. Later a rock regular, a guy who knew much more than I about these strange fish, told me that they tangle you all the time in the kelp that grows at the base of the rocks.

Since that time I have seen any number of situations where big bass used the environment to escape. A few years later, while live-eel fishing from a jetty in Charlestown, Rhode Island, I got a pickup with the bass moving off *against* the current. Given that this current was flying between the two jetties, I already knew that only a big bass was likely to move against it. After a few seconds I hauled back on this thing and I could feel my line catch on something, snap free, get caught again, and then lift unrestrained. It was as though the line was woven into a landfill where it would be caught and then released. I had caught any number of big bass from this spot but had never had this experience. Then I had one last temporary hang-up before the line lifted off. Feeling the power of a good striper, my 45-pound braid broke like a low-cost string. Examination of my line showed that the last 50 feet were filled with nicks, cuts, and dangling shreds from the barnacles on bottom stones. No doubt that this monster had run off deep, weaving my line into the stones—which were like broken glass—as it went.

Along parts of North Truro on Cape Cod, east side, a red weed—a marl or gunk—develops each summer. It's not pollution, but the stuff is offensive to the eye, unpleasant to bathe in, and nearly impossible to fish. Curiously, the moby stripers that inhabit this area most years wallow in the stuff. Only an occasional surfcaster is able to deal with it, because a single cast may require you to spend an hour cleaning your line. Still, during the day, boatmen who are able to see breaks in the gunk often find clean holes where they can let a live mackerel down, then watch a big bass pop out of the weed to ambush it and slip back into the cover. The challenge is to stop the fish before it gets back into the red weed, a feat requiring both determination and stout line. I don't know how many regulars there told me of hooking a nice bass then having it run into the stuff, leaving them in a ball of weed the size of a washer. Pulling the substance away from the line at the transom for an hour, they often found a cow in the center of the weed ball.

There is great adaptability in the feeding behavior of linesides. Some anglers see them as grubbers of the bottom; others, because of experience, perceive our fish as free-swimming, marauding killers that pound the surface to kill their prey. In the former view they imitate the behavior of blackfish; in the latter, bluefish. Big stripers are all those things and more. Many accomplished observers have known the frustration of finding a lineside that will not take. Is it selectivity or a back-of-the-mind knowledge that it is being lured, being fished for?

One time in particular—and I phrase it that way because there really have been many—a bunch of us stood in the flat surf of Race Light while dozens of memorable stripers finned in 3-foot shallows a half cast out. Every one of the people there knew how to fish and desperately wanted these cows. Plugs, live eels, rigged eels, flies . . . forget it. When we first saw them, fins in distinct view, some of the gang feared that they might be sharks. With the first light of dawn, however, it was apparent these were bass fins. Because of the way the fin broke the surface, we had been looking at a part of the tail and not the dorsal. In other words, these dream fish were not sitting on the top parallel to the surface, but standing on their noses, struggling to maintain equilibrium while grubbing, digging really, on the bottom for sand eels. And given the approximate depth there, for the nose to be on the bottom and the tail to break the surface, they had to all be 4-footers! The biggest reason why nobody could catch them, lure them to any kind of a take, was that our offering passed far above their eyes. It was not until a fly fisher with a sinking line jammed a rod into the gravel of the bottom and pulsed a sand eel fly past the

fish that an offer was even seen. After that catching them was easy. Well, almost easy.

This kind of digging, whether for sand eels, bloodworms, sea worms, or even mollusks, is common striper behavior. Fish that have been doing extensive grubbing often have abrasive scrapes under their chins that look like the kind you get on your knees or elbows in a bike tumble. All stripers, not just the big ones, follow a hierarchy of forage; if they cannot feed upon this, they will dig for that. The list of suitable baits is limited only by man's knowledge of what dwells in the sea. I have caught spring linesides with winter flounder neatly stacked in their bellies like pancakes. There was, in the *Providence Journal* of June 1998, mention of a 4-pound blackfish found in a striper. Naturally, lobsters—though it may distress you and me—are found in bass all the time, egg-bearing and size limits of no concern.

At the Point Judith Fishermen's Co-op in Rhode Island, it has long been known that big bass move in to swill on the gurry discharged from the fish-processing plant there. For years anglers simply sat and waited for a dream fish to come along and pick up a chunk of squid that they had laid on the bottom. It seemed like an unfitting way for a great fish to meet its end, but the situation was known to be reliable during quiet hours when dock activity was low or at night when the dock was well lit and few people were moving around to cast shadows on the lighted portions of the water. Known to ply the shadows of the docks, bass fed upon baitfish that could clearly be seen in the lighting. Similarly, bridges present a set of highly specialized fishing situations because of their lights and resultant shadows.

Back when the original Jamestown (Rhode Island) Bridge was in use, a bunch of us hung out there to fish the shadows. Lampposts hung over the southern edge of the bridge and cast a short shadow on that side. On the northern side the shadow was longer, permitting a view of a much larger darkened area. On nights when the moon was full, the shadows were so subdued that we could not practice our craft. However, on dark, new-moon nights with strong tides, the shadows were distinct. Stripers always feed into the current; what happened here was that stripers, big ones, stalked the shadow edge on the dark side looking out into the light facing the current. Thus, on a dropping tide we walked the northern rail. We shaded our eyes with long-brimmed hats or with a free hand. On the rise in tide we walked the southern rail. What we saw were monster bass swimming slowly at a 15-degree angle along the shadow edge and peering out into the current for bait. They appeared as black silhouettes against a gray background. As we watched the whole thing from 15 feet above the water, each hapless bait drifted in the tide from the gray light to the dark shadow, where the black form of a bass pounced upon it. It was so novel an environment in which to contact a great striper that none of us knew how to get one up once it was hooked.

Jamestown Bridge: What we saw were monster bass swimming slowly at a 15-degree angle along the shadow edge and peering out into the current for bait.

When we first started fishing there, we didn't realize the intensity of the challenge. Sure, a few fish of under 20 pounds were hauled straight up on heavy tackle without breaking the line, but the true brutes, the trophies, were way too heavy for that, because even if the line held it would cut your hands to the bone. Walking a fish to shore involved such distance that it was out of the question. Before long one of the gang, apparently through some Florida fish pier influence, devised a gaff that could be attached to the line and then lowered to the fish. At first these novel inventions often bounced off the fish's head; we had to attach sinkers to create enough weight for penetration. Ropes, which were 1,200-pound-test nylon, were strong enough but, at ⅛ inch thick, also cut into the hand. Thus, an evolution in line gaff development transpired, and we finally came up with a grappling hook design with three or four equally spaced prongs, heavy enough and large enough to grasp the Atlantic's greatest striper. Again, after awful losses, we learned the optimum distance from point to clip— 13 inches—and began to gaff fish on the ends of our lines with startling regularity. This was technical stuff. The line gaff and its rope had to be carried in a shoulder bag, with rubber-tubing covers over the gaff points. Fishing alone was dicey, because we had to be ready for anything while fighting a brute fish. Try snapping a clip onto your line to lower a hook, rubber covers removed, while a 40-pound bull striper is thrashing below and your ¼-inch rope is blowing out into the road to foul in passing traffic. One of the last things we learned was that the clutch or bail had to be *opened* once the upward heave and haul began, because a moby striper would often shake free or simply fall off the gaff. Anyone following a fish up by reeling—remember, all of us have been taught to keep a tight line—would either have a free fall or have a rod and reel jerked right out of his hand. Now that we had a workable system for getting the fish up, the gang fished more. It would not have been worth fishing there without a tested, workable means of winning over a dream striper.

Bridge nomenclature was such that we could read where the bridge pilings were, because expansion cracks were placed at the pilings. It was important to know piling locations at a glance, because they often cut 50-pound line in a jiffy. On nights when we found no bulls on the shadow edge, the fish could often be located resting in a neutral hydro where the tide rushed past the barnacle-encrusted piling. Once a bass was hooked it was essential that the angler side-step quickly toward the center of a piling set prepared for battle. Otherwise, the thing could run his line across a sharp surface. It was heavy tackle operated with a high degree of skill and dogged persuasion. We learned of the power of big stripers by fishing for them with brutish tackle while our drag washers bled out the side of the reel in a paste. My therapist says it was a phase I was going through.

Bass behavior was influenced by the available bait. Nights when bunker were swimming the shadow edge, we saw many more fish on the dark side. Even when we saw less bait and less bass as a result, they were often still there, but foraging differently. To us it seemed that more blind fishing was needed. So we just set a pattern of casting every 3 feet in an attempt to locate a stray. Late fall, usually after bunker were gone, we found outrageous numbers of a strange 3- to 6-inch crustacean that resembled a juvenile lobster made wrong. Nobody knew what the things were, and it took me a long time to identify mantis shrimp from my fish books. Stripers apparently plucked them from the pilings like fruit.

Sport fishers notoriously fret over striper population dynamics while giving little attention to the variable nature of baitfish populations. It amuses me to watch panic over the slightest decline in menhaden, outrage over any increase in commercial landings of this fertilizer/chicken feed forage species. It is believed that stripers without bunker will be without food. Even when the notion that they can eat something else in the hierarchy of forage is advanced, the concern is that bass will move on, will settle elsewhere for better foraging. The logic is understandable, but I just don't know if these things are true. Unlike most striper fans, I think the relationship between menhaden and stripers is way overblown.

In the late 1960s we would pick an occasional monster from the Rhody beach all summer. It seemed that the fish were spread, that they lacked concentration because there was little to concentrate them. Then, in 1970, we experienced a dramatic loss of big bass; *nobody* got anything decent. Those who had fished boats in the area for years were suffering the same paucity—until word got out that the big bass could be found in Stonington, Connecticut, as well as in other eastern Long Island Sound harbors. The thing was so out of control that virtually all of the boat fishermen I knew trailered their boats to these harbor towns so that they could snag pogies and fish them right there. The concentration of moby bass, dream fish, was so intense that often it was not even necessary to place bunker in live-bait wells—another newfound piece of equipment of the time. Rather, they snagged a bait with a weighted treble hook, then just let the thing sag until a cow picked it up. The resultant slaughter left angling for big fish on the ropes, because it seemed that virtually every large striper in the Northeast was collected under these menhaden. People who had never caught a decent bass were toting them off to market by the dozens. Fish 20 years old or more were becoming extinct, because they had lost their dispersement along the beaches and in the tiny estuaries that dot our coast. Before the advent of menhaden, it was necessary to hunt for these great fish, and they were doing fine. Now, will you tell me where it is good for a species to have all the menhaden it wants by cruising beneath a school of bait that is about to be encircled by a pogy boat? In resisting the ongoing efforts to run off inshore pogy boats, get them out of our striper waters, they always made the case that they were after fish meal, not stripers. How do you run a net in a circle around a school of menhaden without catching the bass beneath them? You don't. That is why the menhaden were processed in one place and the stripers were dropped in another town, where bass were sold. It is, to use a term in the commercial fishing industry for by-catch (lobsters on a scalloper, for instance), "shack money." These great fish had done fine before the menhaden, a highly cyclical forage, came on the scene. It makes little difference to me who took our trophy stripers in their vulnerability, pogy boat or angler; they were gone not because they were hunted but because they were hounded while most vulnerable—under a school of pogies.

DO BIG STRIPERS SCHOOL?

The widely held notion that the so-called school fish are the small ones is not necessarily so. At numerous, memorable times in my life on the striper coast, I have encountered schools of very large stripers. All fish tend to seek other similar-size members of their species because it is safer. (It must be lonely when you weigh 80 pounds.) Fish hatcheries keep different sizes isolated from one another for that reason. If you ever run into a school of 40-pounders, as well you might, try to keep your head.

The term *schoolies* implies that all schooled stripers are small, which further suggests that we could never encounter a school of really big bass. Just as encounters with high-end stripers are rare, so encounters with *schools* of monsters are less likely. They still happen, however, and I have experienced such encounters many times, particularly back during the glory-day stripers of the last cycle that served as the training ground for me and the rest of the old guard who fished then. When we had gone through a period of intense plug fishing with teasers—a small lure set ahead of a larger one that acts as a casting weight—we began noticing mysterious disappearances of lures. One night, one of my teenage daughters would beach a 30-pounder and I would find her teaser missing. Another night, one would slide up a cow on her teaser fly and the plug would be gone. It embarrasses me to think of how long it took me to fathom what was happening; I guess I just wrote it off as irresponsible kid fishing. Anyway, this tackle was being broken off during the fight because no drag was in place to protect the dead pull between two good bass—one on the plug and the other on the teaser. I didn't really understand this until I landed a pair that totaled over 70 pounds by using a heavier leader than usual. Once my little girls had their leaders strengthened, they started catching nice ones two at a time. We all did.

Teaser fishing will often take linesides when the larger casting weights won't. However, to stack more than one teaser is not advisable for a number of reasons. Mortality is one: There are bound to be more small fish killed when all are waiting their turn out of the water. At the other end of the issue is the possibility of having the same number of trophy bass stacked on a leader equipped with more than two lures. Never forget that if huge stripers are schooled up in a feeding frenzy and it is possible for one to take your plug and another your teaser, then two teasers or more could have you fighting more big bass than you can safely release. One teaser for a total of two lures in the water is better conservation practice and prevents you from fighting a catch that is larger than most bag limits. We will, of course, see such multiple big-fish hookups again this time around; it has already started.

In June 1995 my wife, Joyce, hooked up in the current of an inlet and took more time than usual with whatever had latched onto her. Putting my rod down, I joined her for the landing. Once she had "it" in close, I could see her fish throwing water in the shallows, and I felt something bump my leg at the same time. How could I be seeing one bass over there while feeling another against me? There were two of identical size. The one we kept was 17 pounds. I don't tell you this because they were trophy bass, but because doubling up on what is available should give you a representative picture of the available stripers of a particular time. These were the good ones of 1995. One more.

Billy Gardner, who in 1990 hawked bait and lures for Saco Bay Tackle Company in Maine, was using an Atom swimmer made unique by his painting of red stripes near the gills. Fishing the beach there one night with friends, he and they were catching a lot of the fish of the time—all around 25 to 31 inches. Not trophies, but that term is relative to what is around, what was born years before. He got a helluva hit, with splashing and thrashing that was so violent his buddies had to stop fishing to see what was going on and to help. When the act got into the shallows, they saw that Gardner had two fish on—one on the Atom and the other on the teaser—but the line snapped just before they could net either of them. About an hour later maybe a half mile down the beach Gardner, his pet plug gone, was fishing with a live eel when he experienced a take. When the bass, maybe 30 inches, was landed, it was sporting an Atom plug, red stripes near the gills, at its jaw hinge. Are you still there?

It's common in saltwater fishing for things that are big to be referred to as "big old." Big old codfish. Big old striper. Along with this idea that big things are old is that they don't really move that well—like they can't gulp a 4-pound hickory shad booking through the side of a wave. Too old, too big. (Deer hunters do this, too, until they see a "big old lazy 10-pointer" cross a two-lane highway without touching the pavement.) But *are* they lazy?

One of the frustrations with which live-line fishers are confronted is the seeming reluctance that monster bass often exhibit toward chasing a free-swimming live bait. The experience—fishing pogies (menhaden), mackerel, or arriving alewives—usually occurs when a predator must select an easy target among many. Why would a creature that survives on the delicate energy return of balancing calories burned against calories consumed chase baitfish that are likely to outswim it? If one member of the school is doing badly, unable to keep up with the others mixed in, an opportunity signal is sent to the striper. Live-liners create this signal by placing a hook in the back of a swimming bait. However, sometimes a bait remains too frisky in spite of this; this clearly calls for the slowing of the bait. I have known situations where knife slashes on a live bait not only slow it down sufficiently but create scent through bleeding; this often, but not always, makes a difference. I say it that way because nothing in fishing is absolute. Taken to its extreme, I have known boat fishers who pinned spark plugs—don't bother to gap them—into the shut mouths of menhaden to both slow and sink them into trophy-striper territory. It only works sometimes.

Such great fish have their moods. Many old-guard striper freaks have watched while moby bass cruised near baits without taking. Then, as if by some ill-defined signal or divine intervention, the whopper cut, accelerated, engulfed the bait, and ran off as though it had a prize. One dawn in midsummer, after having been engaged with big stripers most of the night, I watched a New York beach fisherman cast an Atom swimmer into what I believed to be a dead surf. After the big floating plug hit the water, he reeled in the slack, waited up to a minute, then popped it violently once and paused for another minute, a full minute. Suddenly there was an explosion and the guy was on to a 35-pounder. I would have called it luck, but he landed four around that size, fishing the same way, at a time of day when I normally would not even fish with proven methods. It sure takes all kinds.

Eight

Cow Country: Where Stripers Go to Pull on Fishers

EVERYBODY WANTS TO KNOW where they are most likely to find moby stripers. The answer is complex. We can only go by the historical precedents, the record of where big stripers have been taken, to come close to predicting the next big-fish blitz. Even then such generalizations are fraught with risk, because some of the recent monsters—the New Jersey world record and Bob Rocchetta's short-lived

76-pound world record—have been found in places that surprised many of us. Still, I select the traditional answer.

The storied striper coast is an ill-defined stretch of the northwestern Atlantic from Virginia to central Maine. Areas outside of this, where inconsequential populations are sometimes found, fail to make any serious contribution to the take of fish that might vie for even a line-class record. The geographical center of big-fish opportunity seems to fall roughly in southeastern New England, a region encompassing Cuttyhunk and Cape Cod. It all emanates from there in that the farther you go from this center, the fewer your opportunities. Of course social considerations come into play; so little fishing is going on in some sections of the northern portion of this range that it is unlikely anyone would come up with a wall-hanger fish. Maine's angling traditions, with the exception of certain pockets of high interest, largely exclude striped bass, and Connecticut's limited access prevents much of the shore fishing that might otherwise go on there.

Martha's Vineyard is good because fishing enjoys a certain sanctity there, and people are allowed to fish. Places like the Vineyard—and I would add Nantucket—tell us that in areas where striper fishing is a cultural mainstay, more is known about catching them by a greater number of people. Similarly, striper fishing at Montauk, or the entire New Jersey coast, is hardly a fad.

A number of locations on the striper coast have been historically referred to as staging areas. These are places where stripers are commonly found to concentrate seasonally in greater numbers and—year depending—sometimes greater sizes. An educated explanation for this would likely include the large tiderips where great amounts of water are exchanged and where forage species tend to be found. The more water that strokes their flanks, the more ease in foraging that stripers will enjoy. It is not my purpose to name them all, but a collection of popular examples of staging areas includes Montauk, with the adjacent Fishers Island Race; the Elizabethan chain of islands, commonly lumped together as Cuttyhunk; the Cape Cod Canal, which draws upon bait, current, and hungry bass from both Cape Cod and Buzzards Bays; Plum Island, which is really a delta formed by the Merrimack River and which shares attraction with the river; and finally, but by no means intended to complete the list, Maine's highly estuarine Kennebec River. These places are all attractive crossroads for stripers of any size. So once we reach a year when big-fish opportunities are likely to be greater—say soon after the turn of the century—these are the places that will be most likely to harbor them.

When the R. J. Schaefer Salt Water Fishing Contest recorded the landings of the greatest fish of the late 1960s, it performed an invaluable service in the study of high-end stripers. Massachusetts and Rhode Island dominated 50-pound bass landings. Notable exceptions from Montauk and New Jersey probably could be more easily explained by the number of rabid fishers there than by any enhanced

My Favorite Trophy-Striper Hot Spots

Here are my picks of the 50 best spots—boat or surf—on the striper coast.

New Jersey

Cape May

Brigantine Inlet

Beach Haven Inlet

Barneget Inlet (both jetties)

Island Beach

Manasquan jetties (all of them)

Sandy Hook with Raritan Bay

New York

Troy Dam

Breezy Point

Fire Island National Seashore

Moriches Inlet

Shinnecock Inlet

Montauk Point

Fisher's Island Race

Connecticut

Cedar Point and Compo Beach

Penfield Reef

Silver Sands State Park

Enfield Dam

Mouth of the Connecticut River

Thames River

Rhode Island

Mohegan Bluffs, Block Island

Sandy Point, Block Island

Inlet to Great Salt Pond, Block Island

Quonochontaug Breachway

Charlestown Breachway

Harbor of Refuge

Narragansett (including Narrow River Inlet)

Brenton Reef with Seal Rock

Massachusetts

Wasque Point, Martha's Vineyard

Squibnocket Point, Martha's Vineyard

Great Point, Nantucket

Smith Point, Nantucket

Cuttyhunk rips with Sow and Pigs Reef

Westport River

Cape Cod Canal

Billingsgate Shoals with adjacent Cape Cod Bay

Monomoy

Chatham Inlet with South Island

Nauset Beach, plus Nauset Inlet and Chatham Inlet's northern lip

Back Beach, Truro

Race Point, Provincetown

Boston Harbor

Plum Island with the Merrimack River

New Hampshire

Great Bay, including the General Sullivan Bridge

Maine

Saco River

Scarboro River Marsh

Spurwink River

Popham Beach

Morse River

Kennebec River, clear to Augusta

whopportunity. Along the length of the striper coast surfcasters seemed to pick from a spread between Montauk and Plum Island, on Boston's North Shore. Yet over and over the reports cited Cuttyhunk and Provincetown for boat-fishing monsters. Still, the other staging areas often took their turns in the limelight. Even so, the science of where and why huge stripers remains inexact.

It has long been known that there is a developmental progression in striper fishing. People begin—on a testing, experimental basis—by fishing the sea from shore, then progress to ever-lengthening boats. This progression tends to sort the most serious anglers, those willing to make a greater commitment of resources, into the equation. Moreover, they are a more experienced group. (True, I am known for vulgarities about real surfcasters preferring a sister in a whorehouse than a brother in a boat, but that is more a statement of my life among old-time hardcore surfcasting regulars than one of fact.) Thus, one who seeks to make a life's work pursuing large stripers could do no better than to imitate those who fish from boats. The advantages are so self-evident that they exceed the scope of this book and its author's background.

When I researched my third book, *Striper Hot Spots*, I sought to ferret out the 100 best locations for surfcasting. I knew that inlets were going to play an important role in the selection process. Having been a striper writer for 25 years at the time, I had a ball periodically writing about inlet importance in articles for both national and regional publications: "Inlets Are Striper Holes," "Fish the Inlets," "How to Look for Stripers." When I first took up bass fishing, I used to play marathon weekend poker, subsisting on Slim Jims, pickled eggs, and beer around the clock with a guy who used to say that he wouldn't be caught dead with us if it were striper season. Then, one morning around dawn, sagging over a smoke-filled bar, I asked him what the big deal in striper fishing was. He said, "Striper fishing is two things: hard work and inlets. Kid, if you don't know that, you don't know nuthin'."

In researching *Hot Spots* I had to rely upon trusted respondents at extreme ends of the coast about places with which I was not intimate—Jersey, Long Island, New Hampshire, parts of Maine. A pattern began to fall into place: One local regular would pass me to another regular up the coast. And as I went from one respected regional surfcaster to another, I was really going from one *inlet* to another. When the book was finished, I had in effect compiled a collection of inlets; of the 100 spots, 64 were inlets. Even then, many of the noninlet choices were famous because of the influence of inlets nearby. Others, not known to be sea openings, had the qualities of inlets, as with the Cape Cod Canal. What is so important about inlets?

Estuarine inlets are the gateways to the birthing places of most of the striper's food. These small openings connect two containers: the ocean in front and the pond in back. I've already emphasized the importance of current, and stripers that want an easy foraging opportunity need only wait in the currents of an inlet for the bait to be swept to them: The narrower the passage, the greater the current, the better the foraging, and the better the fishing for you. Inlets are gardens of opportunity that linesides can easily find because of their scent of bait and different water temperature. (Estuaries, because they have less water volume, are more easily heated.) It is a no-brainer.

Before I talk about dealing with the social challenges of inlets, it might be best to document the standard tactics of fishing them. The dropping tide, during which water is falling from the estuary, is the best time to be fishing inlets. There are variations in methods, but inlets are largely fished by drifting an unsinkered bait or an artificial, which is cast and then fed into the current to achieve the longest drift possible. Because of the variability in conditions from one outflow to another, this may not be possible in all openings. In some locations methods may be as simple as casting and allowing the bait or lure to swing on a tight line. In places where currents are mild it may be possible to fish the bottom with a sinker. Keep in mind that the tidal exchange is different from one end of the striper's range to the other—4 feet in New York but over 15 feet in parts of Maine. Naturally, the smaller the opening, the greater the currents will be, and the more challenging the angling situations.

In my lifetime of fishing I have observed a tendency for many anglers to unconsciously believe that stripers hold where the currents subside, because the flow of water is too violent for them to stay in position. This is silly, because the opposite is true: The more current, the more ease in feeding for the predatory lineside, which is there to hunt in the first place. For all but the most poorly equipped species, current of the most strenuous magnitude is no problem. You need only watch salmon holding in a swift-flowing river to observe the ease with which they deal with flow; so it is with stripers, even *big* stripers. Still, all such current-adept species seek out sections of outflow where they can hold more easily—against the banks, behind a stone, or at some neutral hydro where they can comfortably observe what passes before quickly pouncing on it. Fish feel all aspects of water movement, and they detect what passes by them through a combination of senses that are a mix of those we understand and some about which we theorize. This *proximity sense*—smart speak for how they deal with feeding on the darkest night in environments so deep and hostile that they would kill us—is how they survive for a quarter century given all the rods and nets hounding them. Sweep a bucktail jig on the bottom of 10 feet of swift current during a new moon—feel your line tighten with a writhing monster that can lift your butt off a jetty rock and go—and you'll appreciate that stripers are there and able.

Superficially inlets are largely the same: They are containers of variable sizes and openings. They are unique, however, in the manner that they are composed of varying eddies, bars, and jetties, all of

which are influenced by wind, tide stage, and even season. As a consequence inlets are a myriad of mixed sets of conditions, and they all
have secrets. It is possible for an inlet to hold fish at a certain distance from the beach for only a few minutes until they shift to a more
favorable hold. Tide change, tide slack, and change of light are just
some of the brew's components, and just when you think you might
have learned some of them, you are fool enough to think that they'll
be good somewhere else.

While drifting a line out into the open sea during falling water is
a standard means of dealing with inlet stripers, it is sometimes advantageous to be fishing an inlet during the rise in tide—a time when
the others are often asleep. It might not be as good, but the area is
all yours. Water is moving, and feeding stripers like moving water.
Moreover, there are fewer complications, given that advantageous
current. With a rising tide, the bass fights the current and you.

Because inlets are widely known to produce good fishing, you are
not likely to be alone at any of the good ones during the season when
stripers are around. Inlet crowds can destroy your chances of landing a trophy striper. Here is how it often happens. A bunch of you
have gathered at the sea end of a jetty to fish the drop. Cooperation
is high because each of you knows that the alternative is sheer folly.
Managed by regulars who appreciate both its importance and how to
accomplish it, a rotation is in play where each takes his turn casting,
drifting, swinging, and retrieving his artificial. Bottom baits are for-
bidden, because to employ them would inhibit all other activity. A
major rule of this game is that when one of you hooks up, he
announces this with a powerful "fish on"; those above stop casting or
feeding line while the fishers below get their gear out of the water to
give you room for the fight. On paper everybody is supposed to get
away from your fish and your line so that you can fight and land it.
Someone is also supposed to accompany you for the landing by going
down into the stones of the jetty, or the turbulence of the surf, or

Because inlets are widely known to produce good fishing, you are not likely to be alone at any of the good ones during the season when stripers are around.

both, and subduing your trophy, helping you land it. On paper, said Mickey Mouse and Donald Duck.

Here is what really happens. When you shout "Fish on," the guy who just joined the rotation—knowing that fish are often taken in pods moving through—is not about to cut himself out of the action by waiting. Rather, he casts more quickly to hurry himself into the action. Then he whispers in his most apologetic tone, "Sorry, too late." The caster below you, knowing that he is at the most productive point in his drift, does nothing, and the person below him drifts longer because he wants to stay with the action. Instead of a clear, unobstructed sea for you to deal with the striper of your dreams, line is torn from your reel against the drag through a veritable junkyard of plugs that are hauled back at the slightest hint of something touching any of their lines. Then, when your line goes slack, they ask you if *you* broke off—when in fact one of them has cut your tight line with his plug. This is fishing with *friends,* and it gets better.

Occasionally, in some hot spots, a we/they attitude manifests itself. The people on the east bank are always crossing the lines of those on the west bank. The boats troll too close. The plug fishers crowd the bait fishers. Somebody casts into a passing boat and, from then on, the boat roars through the inlet, cutting all the lines that couldn't be retrieved in time. Once that happens, all boats are enemy. Just about anything that can be used to define a separation pops into the picture. Before long, warring crowds are crossing lines and blaming each other. Most forget, if they ever knew, what they went to the inlet for in the first place.

If boat traffic isn't too heavy, bass will often run an inlet far inland into the estuary. I think it would surprise many to hear just how often huge bass will risk the shallows and protected back swamps. A cou-

ple of advantages spring from fishing "the back." For one, there are no crowds. When you hit fish in the back, nobody knows it, so your night of fishing doesn't get put on the chalkboard at some local bait shop. Also, if the cows are back there, you are going to hear them slurping and sipping on sperling, cinder worms, crabs, or dabs. (They eat everything: the Charles Church world record had a huge lobster in her gut, and I've caught estuarine bass with winter flounder stacked in their bellies.) In the quiet of fishing these less salty locations, the trap is in failing to realize that the same monsters that they fight out front are now in front of you. A good lineside is going to head out to sea right past that bunch that sets on every perceived movement within 5 miles. You fish these back ponds with heavy tackle, not freshwater tackle. Otherwise you will be begging for your leave to pass those barbarians—and because *you* are not one of them, you won't have a prayer of pulling it off.

It is not necessary to fish right in the inlets, because they often influence adjacent waters. Only one of my 50-pound-plus stripers came from an inlet (even then I was alone), but three came from sandy beaches only yards from a great pond opening. My personal experience may not have enough examples to establish a pattern, but these adventures do point out that your location choices can reduce the risk of losing a monster bass to the structure, shoreline obstacles, and surfcasters from the Pleistocene. You have to wonder if noninlet successes might be more a function of more successful landings than from more available bass. In my memory a number of monsters were taken around me from straight beaches that presented no risk to the surfcaster. It was a case of an angler and the fish—no shipwrecks, barnacles, rocks, crowds, docks, or boat traffic to screw things up. In summary, the fishing might not be better, but you're still more likely to come out with a trophy striper.

Unlike many ocean species, stripers will come well into coastal ponds, harbors, and bays in order to forage around. On our coast

Using a chunked bunker head, Steve Franco caught this 75-pound, 6-ounce trophy in New Haven Harbor in June 1992 less than 100 feet from shore. (Photo courtesy Dick Alley)

many such places are seaports that historically formed the basis for our developing cities—New York, Boston, Providence, New Haven. These ports are hopelessly polluted. Visibility is limited to a couple of feet and the smell, at times, is enough to gag a mule from its breakfast. Still, stripers are not deterred, and many great fish have been taken in such cities. The third largest sport-fishing bass ever taken—

75 pounds, 6 ounces—came out of New Haven Harbor in June 1992 less than 100 feet from shore. It was taken on a chunked bunker head from a small boat by Steve Franco, whose specialty is monster stripers. Providence now has a winter-over population of bass; Boston enjoys some of the best boat-fishing opportunities in the state; and New York is the gateway to the Hudson's very own race of migratory stripers. Why these fish would leave places where you can see a coin in 12 feet of water to cruise such murky water is just one more example of how we raise as many questions as we answer.

An accurate body of knowledge is in place regarding the timing of striper movements. For instance, if a lifetime of striper-watching has taught me anything, it is that I am not going to take a keeper during the arrival of the first stripers. In April, at the mouth of the Connecticut River or Rhode Island's Matunuck or Cape Cod's South Cape Beach, it has long been known that you have zero chance of catching a keeper—unless they lower keeper size to 12 inches. The kind of fish we should be after will not arrive until a month later, at best. Also, the kind that we dream about need every advantage early on to make the grade later. Your fish in May will change greatly by November.

The first big striper of the season will likely weigh less. She will be a great fighter because of her athletic build, but she will not be a crowd pleaser because she will be too lean to pull down the scale. The reason for this is that she has migrated close to 1,000 miles after spawning; this followed a winter off North Carolina, where feeding opportunities were sparse. (Before that, when she had come south, she wasn't in bad shape.) All in all she has been through two migrations, a spawn, and a spring with little to eat. In a Washington State steelhead study scientists kept a fish alive in a tank for one year without food. It lived, but it didn't get fat. Your springtime monster is long all right, but not very heavy. Each month of summer that passes will add to her weight in long-term as well as seasonal growth. Stomach contents alone can account for up to 4 pounds of a 50-pounder. What all this means is that a June striper of 46 pounds might weigh as much as 52 if she wallowed in bait until late October and was weighed within an hour of being caught. One percent, certainly no more, would be dehydrated after 12 hours.

Dream stripers, not mere 25-pounders, are not seen pictured in the sports pages of your newspapers until June. Far less is known about when their season ends, however, because of a host of social considerations that combine with the natural ones. Anglers rush the season in spring because they are eager to begin a new year. Come fall they are tired, and their spouses have spent months of lonely nights while the fishing was going on. Sick leave is exhausted. The ocean steams from the downward pull of hostile, often subfreezing, air temperatures. A sense of finality permeates the shore, where boats are being hauled and towed inland. Autumn storms have hammered the coast making fishing impossible, often for weeks. Some years, just when the water cleanses itself from a tempest, another passes to kill things for another week. And of course it is hunting season. As a consequence, sporadic accounts are often all that we have to document season's end.

Most years Maine's bass are just about gone by mid-October; I've never heard of big fish after that. Still, my old friend and trusted contact for that state, Billy Gardner, once told me that a trawler came in one January with a by-catch of dozens of stripers. For years I watched most of the Cape Cod sport fishers pack in the season Columbus Day weekend, leaving a few holdouts who fished as late as October 20. Another surf comrade of mine, Eddie Mekule, who owned a beach camp on Nauset Beach's Pochet, was duck hunting in late November in Pleasant Bay when he and his son came upon a school of monsters pounding bait. After a one-hour round-trip ride back to camp to fetch tackle, they found the fish still there when they returned. Despite a distressing number of break-offs, everything they caught weighed more than 40 pounds. Who needs duck hunting? The greatest blitz of which I have ever heard, one that I missed, was on Block Island in the early 1980s. It went beyond Thanksgiving weekend—a time when nobody fishes in Rhode Island. One year, in early December, I landed a couple in the 20-pound class after dark in the snow from Charlestown Breachway. I didn't go back that year, so I never did learn when they left. If you are catching bluefish, there is a lot of striper fishing left, and unlike spring, big bass are still around if you are catching small ones. The point is that the fishing lasts longer than the fishers most seasons.

There is a widespread folklore notion that the bigger a striper is, the more sedentary its behavior. "Big old cow, too lazy, too heavy, out of condition" are all anthropomorphic notions that have no place in a natural world populated by creatures produced by millennia of natural selection. To perceive a memorable striped bass as a diminished fighter probably comes from mulling over out-of-condition prize-fighters. A number of geographically dependent factors influence a moby bass's ability to resist.

Having caught any number of large bass in Rhode Island's 70-degree water temperatures in summer, I am sure that they put up less of a struggle in warm water than they might in a cooler part of their range. No question but that big differences will be found between one taken in the 55-degree August water of Cape Cod and another taken to the south.

Less is known of the influences of fatigue upon bass, but all fish are known to produce lactic acid in their blood during heavy exertion. This action could come from feeding frantically upon a forage species that is more difficult to catch and, as a result, requires greater effort. On the other hand, it could be exertion from fighting an angler—or a combination of the two—that alters the oxygen content of the blood. Lactic acid from either of those sources would block the delivery of oxygen to the animal's body and thus reduce its ability to fight on the end of a line. Experienced anglers always agree that there is high variability between fight qualities of fish of the same size, and lactic acid is often cited as a reason for this.

Dream stripers present physical problems that most shore fishermen have never even contemplated. It begins with weight. Even if the thing is dead, there's no surf, and no structural obstacles like cliffs or jetties are present, figuring out what to do could really be a nightmare. Some stripers cannot be carried by some anglers. Imagine yourself staring down on a great fish that you have defeated but are unable to carry. You can't just leave it there. Too many people fish commando-type locations without giving a thought to how they are going to arrange escape for themselves and for the brute bass that is about to be inundated by a cruel, unforgiving sea. Often it is only a case of having a long-handled gaff or 15 feet of suitable rope. Then you can get out first and haul your catch after you're in the clear.

When I previously described my Jamestown Bridge 46-pounder, I complained of how painful it was to hoist this monster straight up 15 feet. On another night, with a bass of comparable size—I later learned it was smaller by a good 8 pounds—I decided against hauling it straight up and opted to tow it sideways to shore. A mistake. What I had never experienced was that the forces generated from sidestepping were worse than those from hauling up straight. I did not know that the human back was designed to deal with forces forward or back, but not from the side. By the time I had towed this thing the quarter mile to shore, I was in agony, and my 38-pounder lay nearly dead on the damp shore beneath the bridge. And I could have used a ride home. These are not even really big stripers, but my wife, Joyce's, fine example approaches that mark.

One July night in 1977 we were picking from a take of decent bass in Provincetown at a hot spot called the Mission Bell when I left her to work a stretch to the west. We had been fishing side by side

Joyce's only 50-pounder was something that no 130-pound woman could carry. All surfcasters don't necessarily pump iron.

so that I could help her with anything over, say, 25 pounds. But now she was alone. I forget how long I was gone, but when I came back, she had a moose of a striper near the front wheel of our vehicle, a good 200 feet from the water. It was something that no 130-pound woman could carry. In astonishment, I asked her how the hell she had gotten it up to the buggy. She replied that she had "inched" it from the wet sand by shuffling her boot feet under its belly toward the shore. Once she was high enough she laid down her rod, got a gaff from the truck, and dragged it the rest of the way. The thing was dead by then and it weighed over 50 pounds. All surfcasters don't necessarily pump iron.

Both of our twin daughters landed stripers over 45 pounds when they were 17 years old, and I doubt they could have put them in the buggy. Moreover, these were fish taken from an easy sand beach. What happens when you've conquered a brute from a greasy jetty on a snotty night when the foam is blowing over the top so hard that you have to stop your retrieve to hold on to something? Sliding back and forth between the waves of the maelstrom, the thing is lying in the kind of water that would discourage a squad of Navy Seals from going after it. Worse, even if you could get your hands on it, could you carry it out? If your answer is that it is only a fish, you are reading the wrong book, and I'm writing for the wrong readers.

Nine

Monsters in the Wind

SOMEDAY, if you are lucky, you are going to experience a major event that will challenge your ability to understand that history is in the making. This has happened to me many times—times I will never forget. Where and when a school of outsize stripers will show is a roll of the dice. Depending upon the year-classes involved, it can happen more than once in a season. Because it is both natural and subtle there are often few cues, little evidence, no ways of knowing that hundreds if not thousands of moby bass are plying the rips of a staging area, an island, some big-city bay, or the spot where you're fishing. Occasionally it happens without detection, or it is over by the time those who fish there have found out. Now and then you are in on it and it is a memorable blitz.

In 1969 at Charlestown, Rhode Island, after a month of schoolie fishing on Cape Cod, I checked in with a fishing-club buddy, Ray Jobin. As a boat fisherman, Ray is the most effective monster striper-man I have ever known. He was keyed to the fishing and happy to

see me because a lot of big fish were in the area. As he spoke, he reflected that I was one of few who deserved to know that the greatest number of the biggest stripers on the planet were in the waters we loved to fish. "This is one time," he urged, "when you don't want to miss a cast, so you'd better get some sleep." We downed another beer in his camper and promised to trade action experiences during the midwatch.

That night, using live eels, I walked the beach with my son; not one other person was fishing either the beach or the nearby jetty. Just before midnight we both made contact at about the same time on fish in the high 30s. Soon after, a flashlight beamed a signal from a boat on the horizon, but I hesitated to answer because I feared spooking the fish in front of us. Then Ray pulled up, mildly irritated, saying that he could see our outlines against the white sand. He advised that we had best head east to the breachway, a jetty-flanked inlet where currents make up strong to and from a back pond.

It was a big-water night with swells pushed by a brisk sou'wester. By the time we got to the end of the jetty Ray's boat was heaving at anchor and he was yelling something—above the roar of the sea—about "millions!" Between us on the end of the jetty and his anchored boat, big fish were slapping incessantly. I don't know if there were 50, 500, or thousands, but they were all drag-taking fish and so plentiful that you could not make two casts without hooking up. The surf and jetty made landing difficult so we retreated to the beach, where we landed a couple of 40-pounders. At dawn Ray's 16-foot Starcraft was half full of fish and he had *two* bass of well over 50—the kind of fish that single-handedly would validate an angler's lifetime. During that summer blitz, which largely went unnoticed by the angling world, Ray took at least six linesides of over 50; Fred Gallagher, who was to later become one of Rhode Island's most prominent charter skippers, had only two because he got in on it late; and Ray Allard, who later became an official of the Newport County Salt Water Fishing Club, caught the striper of his dreams, over 50.

That year three of us often worked the Charlestown surf together with live eels: my late brother, Norman; our friend, Butch; and me. I ended up with two bass over 50, the only year in my life with two. John "Butch" Calkins, a Connecticut State Police lieutenant, landed the best of our small surf bunch, a 57-pounder. I had jokingly sought to trivialize Butch with the idea that he had landed only one big striper, but he was so irrevocably altered by the experience, puffed at his success, that there was no touching him. One of the nights Norman fell over backward when his line broke while setting on a take. Minutes later he beached a 48-pounder. Soon after that he caught his trophy 50 with odd ounces at the same spot where he had come so close a few nights before. We never saw them in Charlestown like that again, and it taught us to make the most of such situations. No one on the striper coast had the kind of fishing that we had. Sadly, we wasted a couple of years after that on that beach always hoping to experience again the kind of fishing that we had known. All our effort, all our will, could not make it happen. That is the downside of having history in a spot: You spend a major chunk of your life clinging to the memories, always hoping that they will come back, and that you will be there when they do. Pursuit of such dreams is an awful drug. I'm sure that somewhere someone else had them.

Provincetown, on the tip of Cape Cod, attracts about equal numbers of surf boat fishermen, who launch on the open beach, and dyed-in-the-wool surfcasters, most of whom come from New York, Connecticut, and inland Massachusetts. In 1977, when we arrived there for the summer, people were already talking about a couple of 50-pounders having been taken from the beach. These landings raised some buzz from the gang, but they were largely written off as a good spring beginning—something that had been seen before. All of us knew that however good the fishing was, it could change any day. Only that season, circumstances were building to the point where just when we thought it could get no better, it did. Early July— usually the last decent week until fall—we could pull up on a tiderip on the Back Beach (the section facing the east), hook a 45-pounder, throw it into the buggy, run to the next point where somebody was fighting a fish, and hook up again. No small stuff, either. It was like a dream.

Keep in mind that a number of angling factors were in place before trophy stripers got there. Surfcasters knew exactly where to look for the linesides that plied the rips between Wood End, Race Point, and Highland Light—a distance of 15 miles—because they had long known that this was something that didn't change. Most of them had been fishing P-town with fathers or uncles since after the big war, so they knew *when* to fish these spots, too. Bass that moved into these rips faced more formidable surfcasting adversaries than any they might have found elsewhere. Remember that this was when stripers were first known to be in decline, and people had largely stopped fishing in most other spots. But P-town diehards—casting plugs and rigged eels with conventional tackle armed with 50-pound line—fished on, because they knew of nothing else that could be done with a summer.

In boats, the fishing is far more productive because the sheltered waters of the Cape's tip provide access to a garland of bars and rips where stripers can be caught with regularity. As the storied location where Kay Townsend and Rosa Webb boated ladies' all-tackle world records in the 60-pound range on the same day a handful of years before, effective methods were well established. Boat regulars wire-lined plugs at night and bunker spoons the size of serving trays during the day, or they bounced jigs that raised a puff of sand on each contact with the bottom. Mackerel, when available, swam with hooks in their backs; otherwise, pollack were substituted. Boatmen jigged miles at sea in the shipping lanes. They used to take their fish to town displaying them on the tailgates of their buggies, which ground the stones of surfmen to no end. Most years surfcasters fished their hands raw at night for little, while boatmen slept in like aristocracy for a much greater number of stripers. Depending upon which group you belonged to, it was either humorous or distressing to compare the two forms of striper fishing. In 1977, however, boaters seemed unable to locate the bass, even the mornings after they had been hammered from the beach. The delicious thing about the '77 blitz was that it was done by surfcasters—the last people you would expect. It had gotten so bad for the boaters that they began showing up at night to fish the shore with us.

One night, rounding the curve of the beach east of Race Point Station, we could see the lines of surfmen in the partial moonlight, many into fish. There must have been close to 100 casters spread along the quarter mile of shore. Many were taking fish off or resting; the fish hit for so long that anglers were too exhausted to continue.

So Near, Yet So Far

Provincetown/North Truro section of Cape Cod, 1960. Monsters in the wind? Jack Townsend had heard about a small school of very large stripers that had been hanging out on a barry section offshore. Quite of a few of the beach regulars had launched their tin surf boats and located them. There had been about a dozen fish in all, and though only a few were taken, all were over 50 pounds. The ticket was a mackerel live-lined over the side after visually spotting (assisted by polarized glasses) those dusky shadows moving around the bars.

No stranger to striper fishing, Townsend's wife, Kay, accompanied her husband in the boat that afternoon and promptly hooked and boated a 63½-pounder using a mackerel bait. They knew they had a good fish, but when one of the other anglers held up a 52-pounder that he had just weighed, their hopes mounted that Kay at long last might have caught the ladies' all-tackle world record. A few years earlier she had broken the ladies' record with a 46-pounder, but it never made the record books because it was beaten that same season by someone to the south. Today's fish, however, so dwarfed their neighbor's 52-pounder that Kay knew she was a strong contender. Real strong.

Once ashore, they spent the first hour showing the fish off and taking pictures. Meanwhile, Kay's best friend, Rosa Webb, accompanied her husband to the same area to fish the same way. Within the hour Rosa boated a 64½-pound lineside within 100 yards of the spot where Kay had caught hers. Kay's best friend had conquered the new ladies' all-tackle world record before Kay ever made the record book!

In case you are wondering about friendships in the heat of such moments: Kay and Jack Townsend had introduced Rosa and Dave Webb to beach fishing on Cape Cod in the early 1950s and they have been inseparable friends for nearly 50 years: fishing summers, living as neighbors in central Massachusetts, seeing or speaking to each other daily. Jack Townsend died in February 1999.

The gale-whipped seas held stripers swimming through the sides of frosty swells like dusky ghosts that departed before you could spot-cast them. It is something to be among a mob of fishermen who are so wiped out that you have all the room you want for fishing, if you can find room to park. A mind-blowing school of monsters—fish so big that if we could have seen them clearly we would have feared standing in the surf—was there . . . big time. Of the four stripers that

Kay Townsend and Rosa Webb with ladies' all-tackle world records that were caught within an hour. (Photo courtesy Kay Townsend)

I had, three were over 40 pounds. Many more of that size were caught, and there were some over 50. The golden dream of surfcasters everywhere became a reality for many that night, if not certainly that season.

Kay Townsend with a "decent" bass. (Photo courtesy Kay Townsend)

Just before it ended in Provincetown, Joyce and I came upon a dawn blitz at a spot east of Race Point Station called the Traps. We had picked a few bass on Back Beach, all in the 30s, when we came upon Joe Croteau's little white Scout. Bass lay scattered in full view all around his rig, a thing I had never known him to do, but he was so bushed from the action that everything just lay there. With the full daylight we could see fish darting through the foam of rollers that built from a left-to-right 30-knot sou'wester. It didn't matter what plug we cast, only that we tightened the line just before it hit the water so we didn't get taken down on a slack line. After three stripers I realized that it was foolish to lay into a full cast; that only gave me more line to retrieve under the strain of a good fish. At this point the three of us were casting 40 feet, throwing the clutch or bail when the plug

Always crowd pleasers, bluefish are major players in the striper-fishing world.

Bluefish have taken a rightful place in the lore of striper fishing.

was about to land, swinging a few feet, and having it eaten. It does not get any better. Then Joyce hooked something that kept her from making any headway, and we all realized at once that it was a huge bluefish, close to 20 pounds. Before long the three of us were hooking them, along with a minority of stripers. It was tiring to fight bull bass and jumbo blues every cast.

The influence of bluefish is another thing about your chances for a trophy striper. It is impossible to fish the striper surf without encountering any number of species. You will catch weakfish, bonito, cod, pollack, shad, croaker, flounder, and bluefish. Still, the choppers are the most common, most aggressive nonstripers to find their

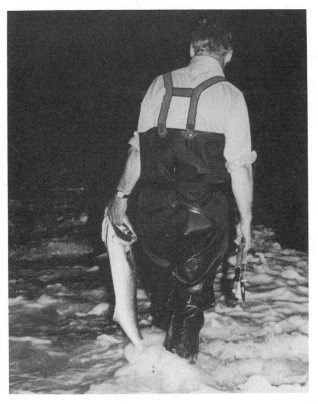

Few old-guard striper aficionados have not at one time cursed bluefish for being detrimental to bass fishing.

way into the fish box. This is so much the case that the bluefish have taken a rightful place in the lore of striper fishing. Few old-guard striper aficionados have not at one time or another cursed bluefish for being detrimental to bass fishing. They can ravage an area's bait supply, eat the juvenile bass migrating for the first time, and take your lure down just as a dream striper is about to engulf it. Bluefish are faster swimmers and frequently get to your offering quicker. They are, pound for pound, stronger than bass. Fighting one thus takes up more of your time and keeps you out of the running for the some-times suicidal first-wave cows. Bluefish are often inversely propor-tional to stripers in population, meaning blues have often been believed to be responsible for striper decline. There is sense in the theory, because bluefish numbers have been dropping off since 1980 and bass have been recovering since '82. In the coming years blue-fish could end up in such short supply that they would have little place in a discussion of big stripers. When I was a boy, my father caught a blue and nobody knew what it was. We blitzed them in the 1960s; few had ever caught that many before. My experience since with seeing the sea often filled with them has taught me to wonder how many trophy stripers have been deprived of a shot at what we had thrown at them by some marauding vibrating-tooth machine.

Back to the mixed blitz of bass and blues. Realizing that I was now fishing alone, I looked up the bank to see Joyce and Joe sitting on his tailgate. They were grinning widely, surrounded by the car-nage of huge blitz fish lying everywhere. That morning, after six weeks of dream stripers, was the last that we saw of them. I should have fished more; it was the kind of fishing that made you wish for grandchildren so you could someday sit back and tell them what striper fishing used to be.

Two things distinguished that season: 50-pounders in numbers previously unknown and a heightened dedication to fishing. None of

There are times when you don't miss a cast, because the opportunity for out-rageously good fishing, this kind of fishing, is both rare and unpredictable.

us surfcasters had ever seen it better. Many who might dispute my claim have since passed away. The late Captain Ralph Gray, a Provincetown charter skipper who in 1958 landed the second largest striper ever taken at the time, 68½ pounds, told me, "The golden days of striper fishing, as they are now called, had an edge in daytime fishing. We were able to bring them up in sunlight on Reverses [meaning Reverse Atom surface plugs], but there was never a time when you could go out and catch forty-pound surf stripers at will. Night fishing that season from the beach was never better."

As a rod-and-reel commercial angler at the time, I fished every night anyway because of the money involved. It was looking at the other blitz anglers that taught me something: There are times when you don't miss a cast because the opportunity for outrageously good fishing, this kind of fishing, is both rare and unpredictable. Who could know if we would ever see that again?

One bad sign, a foreboding aspect of that seasonal blitz, was that nobody was catching stripers anywhere else from New Jersey to Maine. The fish had begun to decline all through their range. An article that I published the following season in *Salt Water Sportsman* magazine became controversial, because people did not believe that the Cape blitz had happened. One of the trophy-striper pictures published with the article, however, included a beach sticker on the rear bumper of our buggy that showed—when examined under strong magnification—we had the year right. Otherwise my reputation might have tarnished. Word of the blitz had unaccountably escaped much detection at the time it was happening, and many people felt that if they had not heard about it, then it had not happened.

Of course all spots have their ups and downs from year to year. For instance, the following season little was taken in P-town—but fishing was memorable 40 miles south at Nauset Beach. I have never heard of a staging area, a well-known hot spot of the striper coast, that didn't crash and burn sometime in its history. That is why when you see indications of resident cows falling into place at some location, evidence that more is going on than usual, the situation calls for a higher level of commitment. It is a case of opportunism.

The mother of all migratory blitzes took place in the fall of 1981 at Nauset Beach on the Cape. It was one of those years when the structure there—the product of some ill-defined sum total of winds and currents—had come out remarkably well; sloughs, bars, and holes were spread nicely along the beach. It was so much a beach reader's paradise, holding fish exactly where you might expect, that a child from Nebraska could have found bass there. One Friday afternoon in late October, a great flock of herring gulls was balled on the outside; they looked like snow as they darted first this way, then that. *Not bad,* I thought. Although I had fished there for 18 years, I had never seen so many beach buggies. Sport utilities were spread the full 11 miles of beach, all fishing. Everyone I spoke with cautioned that the fish there were huge.

In the dim light of sunset I beached a 46- and a 33-pounder, but the latter would be the smallest striper I would see all weekend. A man beside me whom I did not know landed a fish in the low 50s and told me that the night before he had taken a 59-pounder. I really did not believe this guy but began to wonder when trusted friends—New York fishermen with whom I had fished in P-town—told me such fish had been taken steadily, some over 60 pounds. It really never gets that way.

I've seen the exaggerations, the rounding. You can't come away from any kind of fishing without your BS Meter flashing *red alert.* Still, too much was being said of 50- and 60-pounders to be very far off the mark. Andy Mendola, a surfcaster from New York with whom I have shared many midwatch hunts, came to me just before dawn on Long Bar the second night. Using a little freshwater baitcasting outfit, the kind you fish a farm pond with for largemouths, he had caught the biggest striper I have ever seen in my life—60 pounds with ounces. Andy had caught so many huge stripers that week that he had resorted to sport fishing with light tackle for a change of pace. It is not a thing that P-town regulars normally do. It gets better.

Counting the time on the road from Lindenhurst, Long Island, Steven Petri, Al Buccolla, and Petri's 17-year-old son, Stephen, had five days to fish. On the first night out the boy took a pair of 35-pounders that were both larger than any bass he had ever caught. On the second night the boy beached a 57¾-pound lineside. There was less time to sleep before the third night because of a trip to the taxidermist, but they roughed it—and young Petri landed the only striper, an incredible 69½ pounds and the largest ever taken from shore at the time. The IGFA has no category for shore-caught records.

One of the most significant influences upon the average weight of these Nauset Beach stripers was that, without exception, they were wide of girth. All the fish hung deep and sow bellied, displaying girths much larger than you will customarily find in stripers even in autumn. At the time I had measured probably 40 or 50 bass that reached 50 pounds, and I knew I could pretty much follow the rule of "a pound per inch" when dealing with 50-inch-or-so fish. But the bass I saw that season all weighed more than any I had ever seen. The best example is Petri's oh-so-near 70-pounder that was a mere 52 inches long, fork length.

Imagine telling someone to hold off on a 57-pound mount because you have one 12 pounds heavier. That didn't surprise Wally Brown, the local taxidermist, who told me that he had been commissioned that week to do four from Nauset of over 60 pounds. As for 50s, the real number will never be known, but my best guess is that as many as 60 were taken, and many who were there would view this as conservative. Damn, I should have called in sick.

Another time I missed a dream blitz was in the mid-1980s at Block Island, Rhode Island. That late-November circus gave up at least four 60-pound-plus monsters, one by the *Fisherman* papers editor, Tim Coleman. He told me that there was no counting—many

FACTS ON FINDING TROPHY STRIPERS: WHO KNOWS WHAT'S GOING ON?

People don't always divulge that trophy bass are in an area.

Tackle shops don't always know, because anglers don't always tell.

Successes are often exaggerated as well as trivialized.

Monster stripers are not always detected in an area.

Boats usually learn about moby bass first.

Locations harboring giants change from year to year.

The press learns about these things last.

Tim Coleman, the Fisherman *papers editor, with a Block Island monster from the late 1980s. It was the last time that such a blitz presented itself. (Photo courtesy Tim Coleman)*

did not care—the number of 50-pounders taken. All surf fishing. It was the last time that an episode worthy of the attention of history presented itself. If these blitzes teach anything, it is that any angler worth his salt should never let up watching for evidence of an unfolding event. Much of what role he plays in that history depends on how well he was able to see it before it was too late. When large numbers of trophies move into an area, your chances multiply exponentially. What is it they say about when irons are hot?

Ten

Psychological Components

YEARS AGO we fished with a man so in the habit of being glum about the angling that the gang had dubbed him with an unkind, but appropriate, nickname: "Is-It-Lousy." You have to wonder why people bother to pursue fish in a vast sea if they are going to condemn themselves to a life of crippling pessimism the way he did.

People like Is-It-Lousy go to the shore without knowing what the tide will do. They fail to double-check the hooks of their older-than-your-father lures. Their live bait dies. Even if they get far enough to look down at a defeated big striped bass, such individuals would *never* have a suitable gaff to haul their dream fish up onto a jetty. They *never* have a rope to lash onto a heavy fish, either. Programmed to crash and burn, they just don't get it.

For other negative thinkers, the kind of huge striped bass that validates the thousands of nights of effort, as well as bestowing a fortune in human and monetary resources, is destined to be caught by another, because they believe that everything in this world—good or bad—happens to someone else. It is as though they have not been cast in the universal, worldwide play of life. As a result they will never catch the kind of fish that is the lead character in this book.

Few stripermen remain who knew Arnold Lane; much of what is known about him these days is secondhand folklore. Arnold Lane was a legend of Cape Cod striper fishing for a reason—he always caught more striped bass than anybody else. And when there were *no* stripers, he caught only a few. Why? Having spent a lifetime in the surf or pushing off from shore in a tin boat like it was a scooter, he had experience and he *believed* in everything that he did. At the dock nearly 40 years ago—the two of us unloading fish for market, I one, he a ton—we talked about plugging.

"I wouldn't throw that gosh-taked plug out there if I didn't think there was a big striper either lookin' at it or gonna. To me the whole time I fish there's one gettin' into position to take it down. I can never turn the crank on that reel without expectin' the sonavabitch any second. I can't help it."

Successful fishers are all optimists. Ray Jobin—and how do you write about big stripers without mentioning him?—always used to find a reason for, as he would say, "doing a job."

May: "The first biggies is gonna come."

June: "The best month."

July: "Fish, big fish, are settling in."

August: "They get crazy and stupid when fattenin' up on shad."

September: "The mullet run is going to get 'em going."

October: "They're comin' in from Maine where they ain't been fished."

November: "Everybody is tired. We got 'em all to ourselves."

December: "Get one now and he'll be fat as a bastard."

It would be folly to attack such seasonlong optimism by asking what month is bad to fish for stripers. Besides, I'm not sure how Ray would respond if you tried to shake his sense of why striper fishing

is the best thing you can do with clothes on. He doesn't know it himself, but Ray's inextinguishable appetite for fishing is what makes him a success. His greatness springs from the certainty that he will find and catch, because he has always found them and caught them. Ray Jobin believes not just in the fishing but in himself.

This inscrutable psychological component is common among many athletes, not just fishermen, but examples outside of fishing would best be described by someone who has been there. What I know is anglers, and most anglers who consistently do well exhibit other positive traits that cause them to stand out. I grew up trout fishing with a kid who had a way of avoiding the crowds that collected in public waters so he could fish alone long after most others thought all trout were gone. He caught trout long beyond the early slaughter and after others had given up. Years later, we met striper fishing purely by chance. He was still doing better than those around him and still innovating—creeping around back ponds in the deep night in places where few ever thought to look. One time, on Race Bar in P-town, I saw him take a bass while a crowd of hundreds of bottom dunkers were having no success. There were so many people fishing that when you freshened a bait, you had to be careful negotiating the gauntlet of baited lines in order to make your next cast. People were wading out to the tops of their waders and grunting the cast for distance. Because boats often did well there, the notion that most of the fish were out of reach dominated the efforts of everyone but my friend. Knowing that he trusted me, when he beached the *only* fish I asked him what he had done to take it. "Everybody," he whispered, "is fishing in the same place, as far out as they can. I'm fishing alone—in close."

My first years in the striper surf were largely spent bait fishing, and I passed hundreds of nights with many dozens of competent surfcasters. In many cases, however, they fished with more rods than they could handle were a school to pass. One night, one of the guys had two surf rods up tight with thrashing stripers while a third bowed under the strain and a fourth rod and reel were never seen again. I have known others who spaced their bait rods equidistant down the beach—each one with a sinker—exactly 60 yards from the shore so that the same fish saw all the baits while most located none. Worse, it was impossible to effectively tend them all. A hundred rods could have been tended if they were spiked together and fished apart by casting varied distances from the water's edge rather than spacing them along the shoreline. Rod placement is not relevant, but bait placement is. It might surprise you to know how few bait fishers ever think to drop one bait *close* to the beach—the easy place to fish. These examples are not intended to instruct you on how to bottom-fish; they are meant to send the message that a little thought about what you're doing goes a long way toward increasing your catch. Using your head is no small part of the fun, especially when you are catching fish. Another thing about fun is that people who like what they are doing endure.

Striped bass fishing is not nuclear physics. Much of what makes a great fisherman is how he comes to grips with recreation. I'm sure you've known people who work all the time, who get nervous anytime they are out doing some nonproductive thing like playing golf or fishing. It is almost as though they are overcome with guilt once the fun begins. Such workaholics make horrible striper fishers. They quickly realize they have no future on a striper beach.

Then there are folks whose every effort in the surf is an act of desperation. One season I happened to be fishing with a Connecticut surfcaster we used to call Sleepy. On weekends he used to come out on the jetty late in the afternoon for a couple of hours. He never caught much, never fished hard, but I think he liked being a character in the striper surf and he seemed satisfied about how he fell into things. Anyway, he was jigging the incoming, full daylight, tide humping, a moderate sou'wester off his right shoulder when he hooked a good bass. As soon as I realized he was on, I put my rig down and grabbed my long-handled gaff to lend a hand. After a little of the usual give and take, Sleepy brought the thing over the end of the jetty on a good wave only to have the jig come slingshotting over his head. "Gaff," he yelled above the roar of the surf. "Gaff, keep gaffing!" There was a slight indentation with water between us and the end rock, which was submerged. Large enough to put a car in, the space (it shifted from foam to green) was deep enough at that tide stage to drown you. Suddenly the fish was off and nowhere to be seen. He and I were blindly raking the pool with long-handled gaffs while waves were busting and burying us with foam. Finally Sleepy came up with the struggling lineside on the end of his gaff. It was later weighed at 18 pounds.

The kind of desperation that many fishers exhibit intensifies in direct proportion to the growth of a leading year-class of stripers.

There are never going to be enough of such fish for everybody, so the notion of "where is mine" begins to take a positive hold upon the mind. A clear sign is people who have spent their lifetime of Sunday mornings sleeping off Saturday night's fishing suddenly getting religion. Next, they start making bargains with God. (If you want to make bargains with Him, you have to show up in church once in a while.) Here are some of the deals that I have heard reverently uttered, some with long-billed swordfisherman's caps held over the heart:

"Give me one like that one, God, 50 or better, and I'll never make another cast."

"Give me one like that one, God, 50 or better, and I'll never smoke another cigarette."

Of course God should have nothing to do with these people because a) they only acknowledge Him when there are big fish around, and b) striper fishers will not keep their end of the bargain. I have seen many huge stripers caught by people making bargains and those only hoping to do so. Do you know what they do after looking down in the rocks at the 4-plus feet of trophy striper they just caught? They light a cigarette and make another cast.

If 50 years of hunting and fishing have taught me anything, it is that we rarely have a standard by which we can measure success. I have had as much success as anybody, and probably as much failure. I dare not even try to chronicle how many times I was certain everything was going well only to discover that I had actually done rather poorly. Two of us would come out of the woods with our rabbit limits and there would be somebody ahead of us—also limited out— expressing surprise that it had taken us so long. You go to weigh in a monster of 45 pounds and there are two people ahead of you with fish over 50. It's so easy to suffer from the illusion that you really are good. But remember, if you are throwing plugs into a sea so brimming with stripers that you are hauling back on every cast, it's the same way for the others. So often, just when I think I'm pretty skillful, somebody comes along with a reality check. The gnawing sense that someone else might have done better haunts me as a result. Even when taking a hook out of a dream fish I have often wondered if I am doing as well as I can.

Sooner or later all of us endure the agony of standing in a red-hot tiderip where everybody else is catching a lot of fish and we can't buy a take. It is an ordeal that probably has driven many otherwise good fishers back to the golf course. True, early in the experience we tend to blame the situation on luck, but that fades quickly when the man beside you is sliding up his 10th and all you've had is the suspicion

Even after I beach a 45-pound striper, I have come to ask myself if I am doing as well as I can.

of a rub. By then it is richly apparent that those who are catching are doing something that those who aren't catching are not. Among the explanations running through your mind are speed of retrieve, color, action, casting distance, and maybe lure choice. The only thing you feel safe about is tide, because you are all fishing with the same one. That old what-the-heck-am-I-doing feeling soon flushes over you like a low-grade fever.

Catch disparities are a common experience in angling, inevitably inspiring comparisons. You wonder what you are doing wrong and the others are doing right. The guy with all the fish has a yellow plug; therefore color must be the answer. However, his friend, also with a ton of fish, is using a white jig; so it's not color, it's depth. Yet the guy fighting a fish on the right has been casting down the beach, so the fish must be in close. This second phase of the experience, which is equally frustrating, teaches a technique that scientists learn early in their careers: isolate the variables. You know that there are differences between what the successful anglers are doing and your own feeble attempts, but which factors really result in more fish?

At this point it is important to keep your head. (And remember, as a last resort you can always say you weren't there that night.) I'm convinced that many of the better surfcasters carry an ongoing mental directory of things that work along with an equally important list of things to avoid. That's one reason it is obligatory for the student angler to try to come out of these distasteful experiences with information that can be used some other time. Experience is but one difference between a seasoned angler and a wannabe.

Some people are too hard on themselves, imposing unfair comparisons. Obviously, when you're sharing a rip with 50 other fishers, there are going to be people doing better than you. What is it they say about there always being a tougher kid on the block? The numbers have to be examined in a realistic way: If 10 stripers are beached by 10 different surfcasters, the difference in the result is trivial and well within the limits of chance. But if all 10 fish are taken by one person, there is something right about the way he's fishing. And there is even some comfort in knowing that you are not the only one being skunked.

Sometimes the people catching more are just those who are seeking to one-up you. Indeed, such head games are no small part of the frustration of determining what your chances really are. I used to know a guy who had so refined the art of exaggeration that he would end a summary of his vacation catch by saying, "Not bad—I caught three thousand pounds of mixed bass and blues." In fact, his catch could have best been summarized as 2,970 pounds of bluefish. My lifetime in outdoor pursuits has led me to wonder if the world is becoming increasingly prone to exaggeration or if, with age, I'm becoming better able to detect it. For instance, a friend of mine once told me, "We got twenty-nine deer last season." Now, was that "we" the entire Connecticut National Guard? My suspicion that something might be funny hit home when this friend was arrested for picking up a roadkill. I also remember the time when the gang, partying at the end of the season, got him so drunk that he told the truth.

Urged to see an outstanding take of six "50-pounders" on a beach one night, I walked up to a vehicle with some nice fish, none of which was over 45. This penchant for fantasy and embellishment has permeated our culture. You hire a contractor to fix the roof, paint the house, no matter. Here is what you get: "No problem." "Not to worry." "Ready by the first of the month." Sure, what month? The taxidermist who mounted my second 50-pounder guaranteed it for a lifetime, but he died five years later. People, it seems, have largely gotten into the habit of saying anything that will cinch the deal, separate you from your money, impress you about their ability, their prowess. This penchant for writing checks that the body cannot cash skews fishing statistics. If I ran a business, I would never hire a striper fisher. I'm just thankful that none of my kids came home with one.

I've always hoped that none of my daughters would come home with a striper fisherman.

If you ever meet a guy whose truthfulness you question—which is about half the population—and he claims to have killed moby linesides in the last few nights, look at his hands. It is impossible to handle many big stripers, even when releasing them, without accumulating many little cuts generated by the abrasive surfaces of gill covers, lips, and gullet. Only if there are scratches—and they are on the top of his hand—can you be sure he was using live bait.

Sometimes the things people tell us influence the decisions we make about fishing. Say on a Thursday night you can't decide whether to fish the Guzzles near Shanty Beach or the South Shore Bathhouse. If you are 25, you'll call someone and decide what beach to work based upon what you are told. If you are 40, you'll consider carefully whom you should call. If you are 50, you won't call anyone, because you know the information will be so worthless, confusing, or contradictory that it will just throw you off. This book is filled with photos of people who fished a beach about which they knew little. They didn't look for information, they looked for fish.

Surfcasting is an activity that, if it is to reach its greatest potential, should be practiced at night. For those who suffer from a fear of the darkness, this can raise contradictory feelings. You might be surprised how many people are terrified of darkness yet still fish the beach—at night. They deal with it in a variety of ways. There are 6-foot marines with tattoos who wade no deeper than their ankles, and they periodically look over their shoulders at empty dunes. There are people who *never* fish alone, ever. There are those who shine their lights at everything that they are about to approach. Going down to the water—flash, check the shore for sea monsters. Moving the buggy to another spot—flash, shine the light on the backseat for gorillas. Changing to another rod—flash, check for snakes under the bumper spikes. A fish breaks—flash, what was that? A shorebird squawks in the night—flash, point the light into the sky. A buddy approaches in the darkness—palpitations. Fear of darkness is just one more example of how removed we have become from the natural environment.

Many surfcasters are highly competitive because of some deep inner belief that the best of them catch the best fish. Again, I think the rate at which this behavior occurs is directly proportional to the size of fish that are around. I know that in the old glory days of striper fishing, when people were often seen in newspapers with monsters, people fished solely to be seen pictured on the sports pages. The notion that he too could catch a monster bass bigger than the one he saw in the paper has sustained many an angler through wearisome midwatch hunts. No doubt in some cases it might have led to a memorable striper here or there, but I don't think that such attitudes foster any advancement in surfcasting's popularity. Striper fishers are probably a little nuts from the hard hours, the long seasons, and the self-indulgence that seem to be built into the activity. If indeed it takes all kinds, we have each and every type on the striper coast.

In June 1964, while on sick leave for a tonsillectomy, I had the chance to get in some extra fishing—my boss thought I was dying—for the best of a week. During that time of drifting the drop at Rhode Island's Charlestown Breachway, chewing Aspergum between cigarettes, I became friendly with the oddest clutch of striper birds. One guy, an ulcer patient who threw up blood between casts, caught most of the fish. There was another who, every time he hooked a fish, sang the praises of his "great plugs"; in between fish he tried to sell them to all of us. Still another—I wonder why—lamented the impending failure of unemployment insurance. There was also a very silent guy who used to nod in the affirmative when anyone asked "if he had brought them." Other than fishing, their greatest commonality was that they were all narcoleptics who staggered through their days in anticipation of their nights. One night an argument broke out about leaving blood on the rocks; some felt that if the people who fished there during the day saw it they'd think that it was striper blood and it could bring angling attention to the place. While this was going on, a little guy in his 70s in wet sneakers—Sandpiper they called him—went right around the rotation to cast out of turn like he owned the place. While I sought to restrain one of the group from tossing the old man into the outgoing, someone else asked the old-timer if he was planning on *another* swim, so I guess this was a regular occurrence. Anyway, after a nudge, the quiet guy came down with the *them* he had brought in a huge brown paper bag. He proceeded to pass out cold striper sandwiches on thick rolls loaded with mayo while they told the old man—oblivious to the threats of us all—to "screw." Perhaps his worst punishment was that he got no sandwich. Looking east at the mix of fire and pastels that marked the new dawn on a shimmering sea, chewing cold bass with my new friends who took nothing seriously save striper fishing, I knew that the surf was where I really wanted to be.

Eleven

Lady Luck

WHILE SURFCASTING in Rhode Island in the fall of 1988, George Schirmer of Moorestown, New Jersey, beached a 52-pounder, his first 50. It was the best of a pile of bass taken by him and his three buddies in two nights. He later found out that he'd won a brand-new Mercedes in a raffle at home that same weekend. George had bought the last ticket.

Such weird experiences may explain why people love to gamble. We will risk a dollar for a chance to win a million without regard for the fact that the odds are 100 million to 1 against us. We all worship at the altar of chance, because any sport where games are won on a good or bad bounce of the ball can have bizarre outcomes. So it is with fishing, with venturing our time and efforts in the often dismal hope of finding that prize striper. I could fill this chapter with examples of how luck influences virtually every sport, but I'll limit it to something most intriguing—memorable stripers.

In the early 1960s, while attending a Massachusetts Beach Buggy Association annual dinner, I was getting drinks at the bar when the band stopped playing and everyone in the hall stood and began to

GREAT STRIPERS—WHY THEY HAPPENED

George Schirmer—luck of the draw

Tom Parker—lucky

Del Barber's protégé—beginner's luck

Stuart Jones—chance encounter

Frank Daignault—dumb luck

Dr. Al Freed—right place at the right time

Frank Bentrewitz—timing anomaly

applaud. A young man, maybe in his late 20s, came into the crowded hall of several hundred surf fishers and their spouses. He was smiling and waiving warmly to the crowd. *The governor?*, I thought. No, it was the guy who'd taken the largest striped bass ever caught from shore at the time—nearly 70 pounds. This was double the weight of the average striper club's fish-of-the-year 30 years later. Still, there has never been a time when such bass did not lift people off their seats. My dinner was ruined that evening, because I spent all my time following the celebrity for a chance to talk to him, to hear something of what it had been like to catch that kind of fish. Finally, when the evening was winding down and many had left, I cornered him alone. After shaking his hand and introducing myself, I plied him with my questions. He told me that he didn't have any means of comparison, because he had never caught a striper other than that monster. How can that be possible? A person catches the largest striper in a generation and never catches another?

Around the same time, mid-1960s give or take, Del Barber, a Charlestown, Rhode Island, surfcaster, became subject to incessant needling from one of the women who camped with her husband on the beach there and wanted to learn how to fish with live eels. They were part of a highly social crowd of members of the then Rhode Island Beach Buggy Association; they enjoyed picnics, cookouts, and family gatherings punctuated by some surfcasting for stripers. Del, who had held any number of offices in the association and was an esteemed surfcaster, was the perfect person for this teaching job. One evening, as the sun sagged low on the horizon, dozens of beach families were strewn along the shore in those aluminum folding lawn chairs that we've all seen. He walked her down to a gentle surf amid the guffaws and catcalls of both of their families and friends. It was one of those nonevents, it seemed, that otherwise bored people seek to turn into a momentous occasion.

Playing up his part as a competent instructor, rolling his eyes with poorly hidden grins, Del began with, "This here is an eel. That there is the ocean. Now, you open this here bail and just cast it out and reel it in slow. If you get a bite, let him take it for a few seconds, then let him have it with a sharp tug. Here, you try it."

The lady made a so-so cast, closed the bail haltingly, reached down to lift an errant coil of line from around the crank, then complained to Del that she had a problem.

"I'm already stuck. Crissakes, I knew I wasn't cut out for this."

"Take it easy. Maybe the eel is a little too frisky yet," Del cautioned. Then he noticed the line lifting under some unforeseen force. "Set!" he urged, as the line went taut and the rod began to bend with her response to his advice.

By now she was backing up with a severely bowed surf rod while a crowd of silent, intent beach friends formed an astonished gallery along the shore and something peeled line off the reel. Del was grinning with delight; the poor woman was unsure if this was some kind of esoteric beach buggy association prank. Near dark, a breaking wave slid the monster onto the shore of East Beach and Del scurried down to lift it to the dry sand. Word spread like fire through the large slack-jawed crowd that had gathered that the 55-pounder had been caught on a first, first cast.

"I mean, like, what is the big deal? The men put on all this stuff like they were going to a war or somethin'. I mean, ya know, it is only a stupid fish. Like it's not like I'm mad at this thing that I want to put a hook into its mouth and pull it up out of the ocean. I thought I was stuck."

When the mackerel are running, they can draw concentrations of light-tackle anglers from all over. If the macks are tinkers—say under 10 inches—they pan-fry nicely. The bigger ones (I've seen them up to 4 pounds) can be filleted for cooking or chunked for use on the bottom as bait. They are on the oily side but, for that reason, are favored by some fish eaters. Moreover, in larger sizes they will take small striper lures—particularly Fjords and Kastmasters—and even pull drag from the reels of heavy surf tackle. A story that is repeated every few years, one that is heard more often when the big bass are around, is the one about a gang of people using light tackle to catch mackerel. Invariably, during the melee someone is fighting a mackerel when a moby striper comes along and eats the mackerel. Of course the bass is hooked when it swallows the mackerel, and often the striper is landed and weighed in at over 50 pounds. What gets no attention is the number of times that it happens when the unsuspecting panfisher—often, but not necessarily, a kid—breaks off while fighting a mackerel. I have seen these sudden break-offs and I never know *what* did it. Maybe I don't want to know.

An old saying whispered at the altar of luck is that it is better to be lucky than good. Which is fine if you can only be one or the other, but how many times have you heard it said that some people are both lucky and good? Combined, these two traits can produce miracles. Stuart Jones, who became a pen pal after reading my earlier books, was fishing wrong on the beach at Chatham Inlet when he got the fishing surprise of his life. I say wrong because I teach my readers to fish at night with a plug; he was using a chunk in the daytime and not even watching his spiked rod. His little girl, Lindsey, age six, pointed to the rod and shouted, "Daddy!" With 20-pound spinning tackle, Jones beached a 57-pound lineside. It garnered the Massachusetts Governor's Cup for the 1994 season.

Jones's story qualifies for this chapter about luck, because he combines his trophy-striper encounter with a well-honed checklist of skills. He knew how to fish bait, in this case a chunk, which is the striper coast's most popular method. Stu was savvy enough not to fish stripers with a wire leader. He saw no harm in having a line in the water at what is probably the most popular surfcasting spot in the northwestern Atlantic; he was at the beach on vacation with the family anyway. Moreover, once fast to the fish of his life, he did not blow it by pulling against the monster until his line broke. What was lucky about the event was the year in which it took place. That season, few fish exceeding 50 pounds were caught anywhere, let alone in Massachusetts. Lady Luck's best work seems to come when she gets a little help from the angler. I'm convinced that those encountering the most "luck" are those who, because of their experience, have seen enough to be ready for just about anything. When I was a boy hunting with my father and brother, Papa used to say—whenever a grouse rocketed out of a thicket—"You can't get lucky if your gun don't go off."

Combining his skills as a surfcaster with a little luck, Stuart Jones beached a 57-pound lineside. It garnered the Massachusetts Governor's Cup for the 1994 season, a year when few trophies of this size were taken. (Photo courtesy Stuart Jones)

Just south of Highland Light, during a quarter moon in 1977, I had a nice firm take while retrieving a rigged eel. Hauling back, I felt the momentary weight of a fish followed by the give of having failed to hook it. What I noticed right away was that my bait, while still there, was smaller. Only one thing could trim it like that—bluefish. Nothing rips a striper fisher more than to have an eel that has seen 20 minutes of rigging time cut and compromised. I was miffed with a capital P.

You have to understand that this story takes more time in the telling than in the living, that only seconds went by between the take and my suspicion that a blue had cut it. I did not yet know what my bait looked like. Anyway, I kept right on pumping the eel as though nothing had happened, figuring that the only way I could get even was to keep fishing and catch the bugger. The bait didn't go 10 yards before it was taken down a second time in the same retrieve. This time I hooked the fish, and kind of hoped that I could even the score. However, I could tell this was no bluefish. A few minutes later I beached the nicest striper of the season, 51 pounds. Looking down upon it in the wet sand, I just knew what I was going to find. It was a case of confirming something about which I was certain. There, front hook buried deep in its maw, was half of a rigged eel with its lower section trimmed away by the bluefish.

Let's speculate about what might have happened. Had that blue struck just a little deeper, it would have cut my mono leader. With no bait, there would have been no subsequent striper take. Could the blue stalking and taking the eel have brought attention to a bait that might otherwise have gone unnoticed by this fine striper? If so, I should sing the praises of bluefish for the rest of my days. Might a less experienced surfcaster have stopped the retrieve after the cutoff and just cranked in without action? Might such a change in retrieve have made no difference, with the bass taking anyway? What if I had caught the blue—something I normally want to do? Can you picture me gloating over a fine bluefish, say 16 pounds, while a 50-pound-plus lineside—which had started to move toward the bait—had drifted seaward to forage for something with greater appeal and been gone by the time I made my next cast? Yes, I was lucky that night, but many aspects of what happened could never have taken place with a less experienced angler.

The biggest bass I have ever caught, a mere 53-pounder when judged in the context of all the monsters being taken around me, put

Some feel that it is better to be lucky than good. How about being lucky and good?

more fear into me than any bass I have ever contacted. Joyce and I were into an unforgettable take of big fish on Nauset Beach's Refrigerator Hole. Flanked by breaking bars, the hole was dark and deep at this stage of the tide. At first we hauled a few fish from the center, but then action settled into both ends where water was washing over the bars. We both fished at opposing ends with rigged eels. They were all big stuff—none of them under 30 pounds and at least half over 40. We must have put a dozen on the beach by the time we noticed that activity had begun to slacken. Meeting at the buggy, we agreed that we were both getting less. Considering what we'd stuck or dropped besides what we had caught, we assumed that probably every bass in the hole had had a bad experience with these rigged eels. So we switched to Rebels with little rubber teasers as droppers.

With this change in offerings, the blitz fishing started all over again. Apparently the bass, having no experience with them, were less wary of the small lures and plugs. We split to the bars, cast at the same time, and hooked up at the same time. A little later—it was maybe my third fish on the plugs—I had a routine take. Only this time she went, went, and went, out over the bars on the outside, screaming into the dry line on the spool of my conventional reel. I was fishing with 50-pound braided line and a surf rod that was a real pool cue; no shore fisherman could have had a stronger rig. And I'd been hauling on stripers of over 40 pounds for most of the night so I had a fresh mastery of what was needed, yet I was still anxious. At the bottom I grasped the empty spool with my fingers and thumb to stop it. Joyce, her rod spiked on the bumper of the vehicle, was beside me with a gaff, and we were both staring in silence out into the darkened Atlantic. I had never been in contact with anything like this. Pumping the rod and following with turns of the reel, I stored line for a few yards; slowly each period where the fish took line grew shorter and the times when I gained longer. Then we saw the dark figure in the foam of the first wave as she washed up exhausted. Joyce ran down, gaffed her jaw, and dragged shoreward, while I—falling in behind to cut off escape—gasped at the sight of my Rebel's last hook in the striper's vent. That is, dear patient reader, what you call luck.

How does that sort of thing happen? I know exactly. Use of teasers in striper fishing has become widespread. The idea is that much of what bass forage on is so little that small imitations are effective. Moreover, many small offerings can be served nicely with a single hook—which is stronger than a treble but still maximizes the survival rate of returned fish. In order to deliver such undersize offerings, it is necessary to use a lure, usually but not necessarily a plug, as a casting weight. The mistake that many surfcasters make is tying the teaser too close to the casting weight. This does not allow sufficient room for a big fish to take the small offering up front without being touched, even scratched, by the hooks of the casting weight. In the case of this bass over 50 inches long, I hauled back when she struck the teaser and drove the plug into the fish where it found purchase in an otherwise streamlined and highly unlikely spot. Plain, dumb luck.

How many times have we said, "If we only knew?" The year our son, Dick, joined us on the beach while on leave from the Coast Guard, we came onto a nice hit of fish that had been storming the shore here, then showing up there. Each night was a case of hunting them down, and some nights we would not find them at all. The tide was dropping, sweeping water east over the top of a point where a half dozen of us had gathered. It was a little crowded, but no one was in any position to complain while we were taking bass that ranged from 30 pounds up. Dick had just slid a 41-pounder to the top of the beach when we spotted a buggy coming down the shore toward us. All of us had to be thinking the same thing: *What can we do to make this guy think the fishing isn't any good?* If we all stopped fishing, we knew he might pass by. Still, that person—or were there five?—might also pull up and fish there because no one was around. The safe thing was to keep fishing, to hold the spot, so that anyone who pulled up would have to forage for space. Dick, however, wanted to send a clear message that the fishing was so poor we were just hanging around, so he stood away from where he had just caught the 41 (having hidden it in the buggy out of sight). The lone surfcaster pulled up, walked over to Dick's bootprints, made one cast, and hooked and landed a 51-pounder—a size that to this day, after 35 years of fishing, Dick has never taken. If we only knew. Sometimes I think it is better that we don't know.

Sherwood Lincoln, one of the cofounders of River's End Tackle at the mouth of the Connecticut River, was fishing the Cape Beach with Frank Bentrewitz of Clinton, Connecticut, when Sherwood asked, "Frank, will you try the feel of this plug's retrieve? It doesn't seem right to me." Whereupon Frank made a few turns of the reel and hooked a 52-pounder, saying, "It feels all right to me."

Like everybody else with a little time on the beach, I have stung the world record. Enjoying a daylight blitz one midsummer day, I was part of a crowd of 100 surfcasters throwing poppers at bluefish that were slaughtering herring in the surf. People were too absorbed in the blues to be ready for stripers to show on the same baitfish. But because I was wearing polarized glasses, I saw the much larger forms of bass sliding through the first wave. I called out the news to our son. Once we tied small swimming plugs to our leaders—these come close in action and appearance to the bait—we began hooking nice bass. There was one monster, however, that kept making an appearance in the first wave; it moved on a slight angle to the shore to take a baitfish while the bass on the outside pushed in. Every time I saw the thing, snubbing my cast short so as not to lose time too far outboard of it, a different bass would take my lure, engaging me long enough that I missed another chance. You have to understand that in those days we caught so many fish, remnants of an aging population of monsters whose sisters had mostly slipped away, that we could look at a 35- to 55-pounder and estimate its weight within a pound. So when I tell you that I had the world record in front of me, I'm talking about having seen the beast, all 5 feet of her, several times. Maybe the fourth or fifth time that she showed, I hooked a really good fish within seconds of having seen her and was so sure I had her that I had begun work on my acceptance speech to the IGFA. I gave the fish a light drag, not because I feared a break in the line, but because I didn't want to straighten the hooks on the smallish plug. When I beached this striper, I was astounded to see that it was not the brute that I had expected. It later weighed only 43 pounds, but I needn't have weighed it because I was certain that the fish I was after was still out there. And she was. Again, when she slid through a curling wave, I laid a cast where it should have been and hooked up right away. Pulling line from the spool, she went out over the bars into line that my 43 had not even moistened—and then I dropped her. If not a record, she would have been, I am certain, my personal best. He gives trophy stripers and He takes them away. It is one of the rules.

Twelve

When You Believe

LET ME TELL YOU A STORY about a trophy striper—not because it is the biggest moby lineside that we ever caught, but because so many of the lessons of this experience are included within the pages of this book.

It was the last great time, the glory-day striper period so good that we knew—from the writing on the wall— that it was almost over. There were no small fish. When you hooked a striper it was something that needed two hands to put in your buggy. You needed no training in wildlife, no special understanding of the world around you, to appreciate that, with only big fish, the nights that validated the efforts of fishing the beach were numbered. If there was one nit of justice in the situation, it was that those who probably caused the species to falter were the ones who would suffer most from its demise.

A handful of us worked a midsummer beach. Some shared their knowledge of striper movements while others kept quiet, jealously guarding what they knew in order to keep what little fishing remained

for themselves. It had been so bad that only a few holdouts—rod-and-reel commercial fishers—kept up the hunt. I knew the guy fishing nearby was a person with a lot of friends who could swamp the place, but there wasn't a whole lot to talk about during these nights. Midtide, Joyce and I hooked up at nearly the same time and when we looked down the beach, "Jerry" too had a rod in full bend under the weight of a good striped bass. That was really it. Fishing until dawn, we never got another fish. Still, when you haven't taken a striper for weeks, three fish for three casters is almost a blitz. The effect of having (sort of) hit them was like a drug for Joyce and me.

Not that this was bankable folding green, but it would buy enough gas to finish the season. Most important, we had something that would shore up our spirits and lend hope for the next night.

After sunset we slid out onto the beach with some expectation that perhaps a school of bass had moved into the area. We speculated about how they would move through the inlet, and about how they might stall long enough on one of the points that flanked it for us to take them heavily. We discussed whether they would move against the rising tide to come out of the bay, or if they would swim against the falling water to go in. An exercise of the mind—part prayer, part hope, part dream—because they could well have been on their way to Maine or Montauk.

When we arrived at the inlet where we had found them the night before, there were enough people at the beach to make it mindful of Normandy in 1944. We were sick. We had been prowling the miles of beaches north and south for as far as our buggies would take us, night after night of midwatch hunts, all for nothing. Now we finally had a little something to go on and there would be a zillion rods on either side of us. The chance that one bass might run that gauntlet of surf sticks to her offering or mine was between slim and none. To us it seemed so unfair. And the salt on the wound was that we recognized enough of the people there to know where the leak had come from. In the small world of commercial fishing, we always knew who buddied with whom, and these were all Jerry's friends. Maybe the only entertaining thing about standing in the crowd was that among them was an hourglass-figured woman in formfitting waders and guard-belt-bloused parka, hair as neatly coiffed as you'd ever find on a windswept striper beach, blowing smoke from a two-fingered hold on a cigarette. Staring in cattish disbelief, her hair gnarled from a seasonlong dose of salt while living on the beach with limited fresh water—often relying on surf baths and rainstorms—my sweetheart could think of only one thing to say: "That bitch."

At sunset casters spread the rounded beach that flanked the inlet, throwing plugs along with a few eels that had been trucked from far inland. Many had retreated to their buggies by full dark; within an hour there were probably three of us left fishing. Dozens of buggies were facing the water; surfcasters in pairs or small groups were waiting for someone to haul back tight, for a sign that fish were passing. If any of us hooked up, every one of the people who had driven that beach would undoubtedly be crowding our spot within seconds. The lone guy fishing a short distance away from us hauled back, his rod bent, but his plug was hooked on the reel; still, at least half of the gang started slamming doors and rushing toward the water while he laughed at his own gag. Soon the others caught on to the ruse and the surf was nearly empty again. The situation was even more distressing in that we knew we were bird-dogging for the crowd. Before long—and I know that Joyce felt the same way—I found myself hoping that no striper would pass and take down the plug. I called her in.

Having spent much of my life on this spot, I knew what the tide lag was, and knew how soon after high tide the water would slacken. It was a time, I had learned, when all striper feeding positions would change, causing movement of the bass in the inlet. Not that every fish was vulnerable at that time. Still, regardless of what the fishing had been like before the slack, it was certain that those few minutes when the bay and open sea equalized, whatever was there—and it could well be nothing—briefly offered a better opportunity.

The inlet was distinctly deteriorating. Fully a third of the surf-casters had left; moreover, the tide had lost its force. I cautioned Joyce to be ready for a casual, unconcerned walk to the surfline, assuring her both that I would follow and that if any 20-minute span held what remained of the night's promise, it was now. She went first and I left the vehicle a few minutes behind her, just as the last person was quitting.

Casting slightly upstream, she paused after her rigged eel hit the water, then began a rhythmic pumping that caused the bait to slide toward the beach, its tail snaking this way then that. On maybe her fifth cast, with her drag tight so as to drive in the 9/0 Siwash big-game hooks, a lineside slipping through the inlet noted the eel's motion and tantalizing rhythm, pumped toward it, lunged, and took it down. After driving in the hooks, Joyce looked in my direction to be sure I was watching. And I, wanting desperately to provide something to distract the remaining crowd, draped the tail hook of my plug on a guide mount and walked away. At the buggy I walked to the tailgate and rummaged slowly through the gear, looking up through the quarter-moon darkness without raising my head to see if she was still on. What I saw was her characteristic, telltale silhouette, an unconscious habit she has always had of bending at the knees like a downhill skier when fighting a trophy striper. If there were any open eyes, they could plainly see that she was on. The striper tore line from the reel as it ran west, and vehicle doors started slamming as casters began to notice this lone bass's efforts to escape. Despite 300 feet of shore on the right and 11 miles on the left, one surfman cast over Joyce's head and hooked her line. Seconds later, his plug crept up Joyce's groaning outfit. By now there were 30 anglers on the left and 5 on the right. Her striper began to slow in the deep waters of the inlet. A few surfmen came together, illuminating the water with their lights, to untangle a marl of mono. I felt a line across my face from a cast that had drifted my way, and I clipped it quietly. One less. Excusing herself, Joyce had worked her way as far right as the beach would allow, passing the few who were still fishing on that side. Clear of the others, her only concern now was that great fish. It was finning in the inlet, an opening that only a few minutes before had hosted murderous currents but now had slacked. If there was one time to be fighting a dream fish, one time to be stowing line onto the reel, it was now.

Ten minutes later, though it seemed like a lot longer, her monster bass, a fish over 18 years in the growing and a lifetime in the catching, was in the surf. There were no waves now, because the tide had lowered enough to drop the foaming surf far to the east on the outer bars. The water was down to a gentle heaving as it rose and fell softly. Joyce drew her rod back by pivoting at her hips, then cranked as the tip followed back toward the dark form. There was weak move-

Joyce Daignault with a 49-pound trophy striper. All that night word spread about the one striper that was taken in a large crowd of people fishing the beach.

ment, finning that lacked enough thrust to pull line against the drag. I went down into the shallows and grasped its lower jaw. What a fine striped bass it was!

All that night word spread about the *one* striper that had been taken in a large crowd of people fishing the beach—the only known hit. Surfmen stopped by to see the fish and to congratulate her. Though not her largest, it was her most memorable trophy striper because, unlike many that we encounter, it was the product of some inscrutable faith in what we do. At 49 pounds it had taken a favorite bait, though we will never know if it might have taken anything else. That is the thing about a great striped bass. What defines its greatness? Wouldn't it be simplistic to try to define an unforgettable striper by size alone? More importantly, what is it about the encounter that defines it as momentous for us? Are we lucky or are we good?

A curious repetition is occuring today of a time in the past when we had a life on the striper coast—when one summer was so much like another in those years on the beaches that I find it difficult to recall whether my wife's first big night was four 30-pounders or three 40-pounders. The biggest bass seem to be the only way that I am able to control the passage of time, to put a handle on who caught what, in which years. Once the kids could walk, we tossed the four of them on a mattress in the back of a station wagon and fished deep into the night. Each of us could make a surf rod talk and a fly rod whisper. We cast our manic lines into any salty trickle that could find the sea east of Cape May, from the Connecticut to the Kennebec. If anyone dared to breathe a word of striped bass amid the scent of stale beer in some waterfront tavern, our lines soon swept the current there. It was a time when squid stink and salt spray were so much a part of our lives that we didn't know they were there. It was not always high drama, though the memory has room for only the good nights, but

We cast our manic lines into any salty trickle that could find the sea east of Cape May, from the Connecticut to the Kennebec.

the expectations never let up. Haunted by what we just knew had to be there, our belief that a trophy striper was imminent fueled our vitality and shored up our often flagging spirits. Great stripers have always been the stuff of legends. They were to us mystical shadows as ethereal as the early-morning fog that danced upon the sea at our fore. We had, after a lifetime of midwatch hunts, learned the keys to the striper strongholds.

Now, with stripers back, the situation full circle, it probably will happen to you, dear patient reader. That same squid stink and salt spray will course through your veins as well. It's your turn to mumble and stagger through many sleepless seasons looking for a greater God than surfcasting, that trophy striper that haunts your dreams. Like you, we started with small fish and grew with the ones that we had not killed. Like us, you will make the mistake of believing that once you catch *your* trophy striper, some inscrutable goal will have been reached and the madness will end. It won't, because just as there is always a taller mountain, there is always a bigger bass. I can tell you that life in the high surf is a dangerous drug that will wake you from your dreams in the deep night sweating, fearing that someone is out there on some lonely beach doing it without you. It never lets up. When bass are in your dreams, they curse your life to a study in fluids; you won't move a spoon through the cornflakes without flashbacks. You will slow while driving over bridges and tarry in the passing of even the smallest creeks because, to a striper addict, wherever there is water there is promise. Given the chance, you will learn that time is measured in tide and that what makes tonight different from last is some small change in wind, some triviality that no outsider could ever begin to understand. If history is any teacher, you will become accustomed to fishing until you drop and only eating when there is time. You will learn to label hot spots without names, then tell no one where they are. Given the time, your sanity will come into question, if not by others then certainly by the person shuffling in your boots. It is a sure sign of trouble when you begin measuring the seasons by which way the stripers are going on the beach or defining them by whether the cod on your line indicate it's too early or too late to fish for bass. The winds, in their prevalence, will warn of whatever message of the seasons you might have missed. Sadly, whatever you know of the world around you will explain itself only in terms of striped bass and be understood only by those of your ilk. Then you will know enough of this universal malaise to feel sorry for those who do.

Still, if I could do it all over again, I would play it the same way because little else in life has real meaning. Anything that does is so fleeting that it pales in the shadow of our adventures. It is all a game, and as games go we could all do worse than to chase a dream, a trophy striper.

About the Author

FRANK DAIGNAULT'S articles have appeared in national and regional outdoor publications since 1970. This is his fourth book on striper fishing. While primarily a striper writer, he has also published widely on fly fishing for trout and salmon as well as upland hunting and shooting. He has lectured on fishing and hunting for outdoor exhibitions and sportsmen's clubs since 1979.

Daignault has picked blueberries and night crawlers, trapped for furs, worked as a floor boy in a woolen mill, and was a navy yeoman. Serving his apprenticeship at Pratt and Whitney Aircraft, he has been employed as an aircraft machinist and also as a marine mechanic in the Polaris Missile Program. He earned his master's degree in industrial education at age 41 from Rhode Island College. His last tour in the real world was as a teacher of technical education in Johnston, Rhode Island, from which he retired in 1989 after 23 years.

Daignault fishes and hunts with his wife, Joyce, out of Millville, Massachusetts, as the song goes, "eight days a week."

Index

Note: **Bold** page numbers indicate information in sidebars; *italic* page numbers indicate pictures.